THE VISION OF GOD

VLADIMIR LOSSKY

THE VISION OF GOD

Translated by
ASHELEIGH MOORHOUSE

Preface by
JOHN MEYENDORFF

ST. VLADIMIR'S SEMINARY PRESS
CRESTWOOD, NEW YORK 10707
1983

A selection of books in the English language
by the same author

THE MYSTICAL THEOLOGY OF THE EASTERN CHURCH
(1944; 1957; 1976)

THE MEANING OF ICONS by V. Lossky and Leonid Ouspensky
(1952; 2nd revised ed. 1982; 3rd printing 1983)

THE IMAGE AND LIKENESS OF GOD
(1967; 1974)

ORTHODOX THEOLOGY: AN INTRODUCTION
(1978)

Library of Congress Cataloging in Publication Data

Lossky, Vladimir, 1903-1958.
    The vision of God.

    Translation of: Vision de Dieu.
    Includes index.
    1. Beatific vision—History of doctrines.   2. God—
History of doctrines.   3. God—Knowableness—History of
doctrines.   I. Title.
BT98.L6313   1983   231   83-20220
ISBN 0-913836-19-2

THE VISION OF GOD

First published in English in 1963
Second edition 1973

ISBN 0-913836-19-2

PRINTED IN THE UNITED STATES OF AMERICA
BY
ATHENS PRINTING COMPANY
NEW YORK, N. Y.

Contents

Preface

Among Orthodox theologians of our generation Vladimir Lossky was one who sought to present Orthodoxy to the West not just as the historic form of Eastern Christianity, but as permanent and catholic truth. This witness was the major concern of his life and led him to work in two fields complementary in spirit: Byzantine theology, the organic continuation of the tradition of the Greek Fathers; and the Latin Middle Ages, where he sought, notably in Meister Eckhart, possible points of contact with the Orthodox East.

This double interest was a continuation on a strictly scientific plane of the tradition of the best academic circles of old St. Petersburg, to which the Lossky family belonged, a tradition which had produced not only great Byzantine scholars but also medievalists of note. But it was the spiritual aspect of the schism between East and West which led Lossky into the path which he followed in his work as a scholar and theologian. The points which seemed to him to divide most Christians attracted his attention in the highest degree—the doctrine of the procession of the Holy Spirit, and the doctrine of the uncreated energies of God—and, in all his writings, one is constantly aware of the double intention of preserving the integrity of Orthodoxy while maintaining a dialogue with the Christian West.

As a controversialist and apologist, Vladimir Lossky was sometimes intransigent and harsh. However, in the last years of his life one sees him developing more and more that serene wisdom which made his personality so engaging, and Etienne Gilson could write in his preface to the posthumous edition of Lossky's doctoral thesis on Eckhart: "A kind of peace radiated gently from this man who was so modest, so perfectly simple and good, whose secret was perhaps to incarnate among us the Christian spirit itself, and to do so as if by virtue of an almost natural vocation."

In his book on *The Mystical Theology of the Eastern Church,* which has become a virtual classic, Vladimir Lossky gives a systematic exposition of what theology was for the Fathers; the contemplation of God and at the same time the expression of the Inexpressible. The thought of St. Gregory Palamas on the essence and energies of God already occupies a central place in this work.

The series of lectures on "The Vision of God," which we are now publishing in the Orthodox Library and which was given at the Ecole pratique des Hautes Etudes (5th section) at the Sorbonne in 1945-6, is of a more historical nature and is presented above all as a patristic introduction to what has been called "Palamism."

Having worked ourselves to "introduce" Palamas to the western reader, we hasten to confess here the special and personal pleasure which we experienced in reading Lossky's manuscript and in discovering there, treated in a manner infinitely more elegant and thorough than we could have achieved, an aspect of the problem which we have not dealt with in detail: the patristic origins of the terminology of Palamas. In preparing his lectures Lossky certainly ignored recent works, notably that of P. Sherwood on St. Maximus the Confessor, which would have helped to clarify his thought even more; but his exceptional erudition and scrupulosity give his book an incontestable value. The very evident tendency in Lossky to integrate the theology of grace into a soteriological and also of course Christological, ecclesiological and sacramental context, is particularly welcome. This new accent was inevitable in an exposition of the general thought of the Greek Fathers on the vision of God and deification. It is, in fact, impossible to understand fully the theology and formulae of Palamas with reference only to the Cappadocians and Pseudo-Dionysius; it is by way of the post-Chalcedonian Christology and St. Maximus the Confessor that we are truly led to the ultimate developments of Byzantine theology.

As a historian of thought and as a theologian, Lossky invites us here to a dialogue, a dialogue which would really go to the bottom of things and would seek the truth which unites and liberates, which is neither Byzantine nor Latin, but whose one source is "the Spirit of truth who proceeds from the Father."

— *John Meyendorff*

CHAPTER ONE

The Tradition of the Fathers and Scholasticism

We propose to study the question of the vision of God as it has been posed in Byzantine theology.

This subject may appear too vast: vision meaning knowledge, and knowledge of things divine being the definition of theology as a whole. It is a matter then of stating precisely what will be the object of our research.

No Christian theologian has ever denied *ex-professo* that the elect will have a vision of God in the state of final beatitude. This is a truth formally attested by the Scriptures: "We shall see him as he is," ὀψόμεθα αὐτὸν καθὼς ἐστιν (1 John 3: 2). However, it has given rise to different theological developments, all the more so in that the same Scriptures, the same Epistle of St. John (4: 12) asserts that "no one has ever seen God," θεὸν οὐδεὶς πώποτε τεθέαται, and St. Paul states precisely that He cannot be seen (1 Tim. 6: 16). The question has been raised whether this vision of God is reserved exclusively for eternal life, *in patria*, or if it can in fact begin here, *in via*, in the ecstatic experience. Insofar as it concerns a face to face vision in the age to come, it has been interpreted as one of the characteristics of union with God or indeed as the origin of beatitude itself, the beatific vision presenting itself then as the ultimate goal for human beings. Finally, as for the actual object of this vision of God *sicuti est*, καθώς ἐστιν, doctrinal interpretation has differed, depending on whether the possibility of knowing the divine essence is admitted or, on the contrary, whether its absolute unknowable nature for created beings is affirmed. It is especially this last question which we intend to keep in mind in the course of our examination of the doctrines of several Byzantine theologians concerning the vision of God.

If the essence of God is unknowable by definition, how will we be able to know God as He is, according to the word of St. John? On the other hand, if in the age to come His essence is to be an object of beatific knowledge for created intellects, in what sense must we conceive the unknowable nature of God as affirmed by the Scriptures? The dissimilar solutions which this problem has found among eastern and western theologians suggests that we are dealing with differing theories of mystical knowledge based on ontologies that are not always the same for the Byzantine East and the Latin West.

In the fourteenth century the question of the beatific vision was raised in the East and in the West independently and in different doctrinal contexts. In Byzantium it was the occasion for disputes over the real distinction between the divine essence and the divine energies. The Councils of Constantinople of 1341, 1351 and 1368 affirm, among other things, that God lives absolutely inaccessible insofar as His essence is concerned, which cannot be the object of knowledge or vision even for the blessed and the angels, to whom the Divine Being is revealed and has become knowable in His uncreated and deifying energies. In Rome, or rather in Avignon, the question of the beatific vision was raised in a different way. It simply involved the question whether the elect could enjoy the vision of the divine essence after death and before the last judgment, or whether this bliss was reserved for the state of final beatitude after the resurrection. Pope Benedict XII, in his constitution *Benedictus*

Deus of January 29, 1336, censuring the opinion of his predecessor John XXII, according to whom the face to face vision of God would take place only after the resurrection, has this to say among other things: "... after the passion and death of our Lord Jesus Christ, they (the elect) will see and do see the divine essence in an intuitive and face to face vision, without any created intermediary which would interpose itself as an object of vision, the divine essence appearing to them immediately, without a veil (*nude*), clearly and openly; so that in this vision they might enjoy the divine essence itself." Five years later, in 1341, the same Benedict XII, examining the doctrine of the Armenians who were seeking union with the Church of Rome, reproached them—among other erroneous opinions—for having denied to the blessed the intuitive vision of the essence of God.

We find ourselves confronted by two formulae neatly opposed, the first of which resolutely denies all possibility of knowing the essence of God, while the second explicitly insists on the fact that it is the actual essence of God which must be the object of beatific vision. However, in spite of their contradictory character, these two doctrines agree in that they wish to see God as He is, face to face, without any created intermediary. One may wonder if this contradiction between the eastern and western doctrines of the vision of God, as it exists in the definitions of the fourteenth century, is due simply to a difference of terminology, or if there is after all a basic difference in theological conception. In order to answer this very delicate and complex question a parallel study would have to be made of the eastern and western doctrines, concentrating especially on the notion of the divine essence in Latin scholasticism. I hope to be able to approach this problem later, but for the moment we will remain within the limits we have assigned to our work, devoted as it is to the study of Byzantine theology.

We will therefore leave to one side the development of the doctrine of the vision of God "in His essence" in western theology. Let us simply note that this doctrine had been fully elaborated and expressed in very precise terms well before it was formulated in the magisterial decree of Pope Benedict XII to which all theologians of later periods usually refer. St. Thomas Aquinas presents this doctrine of the *visio beata* in several of his works, especially in a long discourse on the beatitude of beings endowed with intelligence, in his *Summa contra Gentiles* (III 51, 54, 57). In the *Summa Theologica* the first part, Question 12, *Quomodo deus cognoscatur a nobis,* is almost entirely devoted to the vision by created intellects of the divine essence. In the first article of Question 12 (*utrum aliquis intellectus creatus possit Deum per essentiam videre*—"Is a created intellect able to see God in essence?"), St. Thomas, beginning with the objections to his thesis, following the custom of the scholastic *quaestiones,* cites two eastern theological authorities. He says: *Videtur quod nullus intellectus creatus possit Deum per essentiam videre,* "It seems that no created intellect can see God in essence," and *Chrysostomus enim, super Ioan. (Hom. XV) exponens illud quod dicitur Ioan. I (18) Deum nemo vidit unquam, sic dicit: Ipsum quod est Deus, non solum prophetae, sed nec angeli viderunt, nec archangeli. Quod enim creabilis est naturae, qualiter videre poterit quod increabile est?* "Chrysostom, in his fifteenth Homily on St. John, explains the passage from John 1: 18: No one has ever seen God, saying: This signifies that God has not been seen by the prophets, nor even by the angels and archangels. For how can that which is created nature see that which is uncreated?" The second authority is drawn from Dionysius the Areopagite, *De divinis nominibus,* Chapter I (5): *Neque sensus est ejus, neque phantasia, neque opinio, nec ratio, nec scientia,* "He cannot be known by the senses, nor in an image, nor by opinion, nor by reason, nor by knowledge." St. Thomas replies to this objection, based as it is on the texts of St. John Chrysostom and Dionysius, noting that the two Greek authorities agree more on the incomprehensibility than on the unknowable nature of the divine essence: *Dicendum quod utraque auctoritas loquitur de visione comprehensionis.* In effect, though God's essence can be seen by created intellects in the state of beatitude, it will never be fully understood. This distinction between the vision of knowledge and the vision of comprehension will become a commonplace in scholasticism and will be used to interpret the texts of the Fathers—especially of the Greek Fathers—which seem hard to reconcile with the doctrine of the vision of God in essence.

However, in more recent times some commentators on the *Summa Theologica* wondered if the doctrine of certain Greek Fathers, above all that of St. John Chrysostom as quoted by St. Thomas, could actually be reconciled with the idea of the vision of the divine essence found among the scholastic theologians of the West.

This question was posed in a radical way by the Jesuit scholar Gabriel Vasquez (1551-1604),[1] who taught theology in Spain and at Rome. In his *Commentaries and Discourses* on the first part of the *Summa Theologica,* in Discussion XXXVII,[2] while expounding the doctrine of the vision of God in created intellects, Vasquez mentions the error of the Armenians and Greeks who in recent times (*recentiorum graecorum*) deny even to the blessed the possibility of clearly seeing God in essence. According to this erroneous doctrine God cannot be seen in Himself, but only in His likeness or the light derived from Him (*tantum per quandam similitudinem, aut lucem ab eo derivatam*). Some claim that Abelard taught the same error, although St. Bernard says nothing about it in his letter of accusation against the philosopher. This doctrine is also imputed to his disciple Arnold of Brescia, and likewise to Amalric of Bena and the Albigensian heretics. But what is especially important, according to

---

[1]Gabriel Vasquez, *Bellomontanus theologus*, S.J. *Commentaria ad disputationes in primam partem S. Thomae*, Vol. 1, Antwerp, 1621.

[2]pp. 195-200: *Disputatio* XXXVII: *An visio Dei sicuti est, intellectui creato possit a Deo communicari.*

Vasquez, is that some of the greatest of the Fathers of the Church seem to have been very close to this opinion (*non longe ab hac sententia fuisse videntur nonulli ex gravioribus Ecclesiae Patribus*). Vasquez begins by advancing the teaching of St. John Chrysostom on the unknowable nature of the divine essence. Examining in context the passage from this Father quoted by St. Thomas, citing other texts from Chrysostom (taken especially from the homilies on "the incomprehensible nature of God"), he strives to show that it is not a matter with him of incomprehensibility in the scholastic sense of the term, but indeed of the absolute impossibility of knowing God in His essence. St. Thomas, he says, is trying to defend Chrysostom and the other Fathers who followed his opinion, or who taught as he did on the unknowable nature of the essence of God, by interpreting them in the good sense. But this sense is indefensible for Vasquez. "We can prove with evidence," he says, "that the doctrine of the Fathers (against the knowable nature of the essence) must not be understood in the sense of vision which the scholastics call comprehension, but in fact in the sense of a full, clear and intuitive idea of God as He is." Vasquez goes so far as to justify, in a certain measure, the thesis of Eunomius who maintained, in the fourth century, the full comprehensibility of the essence of God for the human intellect. "Eunomius was after all not mad," says Vasquez, "in maintaining that the idea he could have of God was equal to the idea and knowledge God has of Himself. The equality of knowledge which he upheld as opposed to the Fathers was related solely to the object of this knowledge. He meant that the whole formal content of the divine nature, since it formed the object of divine knowledge, could also be seen by himself, Eunomius. But this must necessarily by conceded to the blessed who see God as He is, for all that is in God formally is God, being identical with His essence; therefore nothing that is in God and forms the object of His knowledge can remain hidden to the blessed." In this transposing of Eunomius' rationalistic doctrine of knowledge on to a mystical plane, i.e., into the intuitive vision of the blessed, Vasquez assimilates it to the scholastic doctrine of the vision of the divine essence in the glorified state, and accuses the Fathers of having denied the possibility of knowing God as He is. As a result it is not only St. John Chrysostom who would profess this error, according to Vasquez, but also St. Basil, St. Gregory of Nyssa, St. Cyril of Alexandria, Theodoret, St. John Damascene and others. The only exceptions among the Greek Fathers, according to Vasquez, would be Origen, St. Gregory Nazianzus and Dionysius the Areopagite. All the rest are guilty of having held an erroneous opinion about the unknowable nature of the essence of God. Among the Latin Fathers, Vasquez accuses St. Ambrose, St. Jerome, Primasius and Isidore of Seville of having professed the same error.

In contrast to the scandal of this accusation, other western theologians contemporary to Vasquez seek to excuse the Fathers by returning to St. Thomas' distinction between the unknowable nature of the divine essence and its incomprehensibility. The Fathers did not deny the clear and intuitive vision of the essence of God, but only the possibility of comprehending it, just like the scholastic theologians. There is therefore no reason for opposing the thought of the Fathers, in particular the Greek Fathers, to scholastic theology, in this question of the vision of God. Such is the point of view of Francisco Suarez (1548-1617),[3] who tries to interpret the texts of the Fathers quoted by Vasquez in the sense of the impossibility of a comprehensive vision, such as God alone can have of Himself. He has some reservations about St. John Chrysostom, who expresses himself in a most obscure and difficult manner (*Chrysostomus obscurius et difficilius loquitur*). This is why some modern theologians (Suarez does not name them, but we know that he is thinking especially of Vasquez) are unwilling to admit any other

---

[3]*De Deo*, I. 11, c. VII, no. 15-19, Mainz, 1607.

interpretation and strive only to convict Chrysostom of error, while also regarding several other Fathers of the Church in the same light. It seemed incredible to Suarez that an error so obvious and so contrary to the Scriptures could have received the common assent of so many Fathers; this would have been an intolerable fault (*intolerabilis lapsus*). Even in Chrysostom, according to Suarez, one can find passages which mitigate his intransigent position and permit an interpretation of the vision of the divine essence which he refuses to created beings in the scholastic sense of *visio comprehensiva*. Besides, the rigorous nature of the negative expressions can be very well explained by his polemical outburst against the Anomoeans, as the inevitable exaggeration of debate, giving the impression that the Fathers were falling into an opposite extreme in their fight against the thesis of the heretics.

Another commentator of St. Thomas, the Jesuit Father Diego Ruiz de Montoya (1562-1632),[4] joins Suarez in rejecting the accusation which Vasquez had hurled against the Fathers. "Among the most diligent and most noble authors of our time," he says, "there are some who claim that the Fathers we have just cited refused in an absolute way—both to angels and to the blessed—all possibility of seeing the substance of God as He is, asserting that the angels and the blessed can see nothing but an effect extraneous to God, not God Himself" (*quasi videatur ab illis aliquis alius effectus Dei, et non ipse Deus*). This is what Vasquez is trying to prove. Ruiz undertakes a defense of the Fathers: "It is impossible that the best and largest part of the Church should have fallen into error, especially into an error so gross and obvious" (*errore valde crasso et manifesto*). Evidently it would be a contradiction of the Scriptures and a denial of the face to face vision to assert that the object of the beatific vision is not God Himself, but only an effect of God. While

---

[4]Didace (=Diego) Ruiz, *De scientia Dei,* disput. VI, sctn. VII, Paris, 1629.

examining the passages of the Greek Fathers quoted by Vasquez, Ruiz seeks to ward off the accusation of such a flagrant error. If St. Cyril of Jerusalem asserts that the angels see God "according to their capacity," this is not yet a negation of the vision of God *simpliciter et omni modo*. The Fathers are refusing to creatures that comprehension of God which they attribute to God alone. Now, this is precisely the thesis of Ruiz, in his sixth *Disputatio*, where he asserts that "divine science alone has a comprehension of God." Vasquez defends another thesis: that it is possible for a created intellect to know God as He is. The tasks of these two Jesuit theologians are different and almost contrary. This is why the patristic texts which present a difficulty for Vasquez serve to support the thesis of Ruiz de Montoya.

The distinction between knowledge and comprehension is too subtle. In affirming knowledge of God while denying comprehension, we can enter into either meaning; while affirming knowledge we may concede too much to comprehension, to the point that—like Vasquez—we may find ourselves defending the Anomoeans, or while opposing comprehension we may seek to limit knowledge, as in the case of Ruiz.

What is comprehension in the strict sense of the word? Ruiz refers to St. Thomas: to comprehend means to know perfectly. Now an object is known perfectly when it is known to the extent that it is knowable (Pt. I, q. 12, art. 7). It is clear that God alone can have comprehension, i.e., the adequate knowledge of Himself, for His unknowable nature, being uncreated, requires an uncreated knowledge, something a created intellect cannot have. Therefore the beatific vision will never be able to give comprehension of God, for, while having the divine essence as its formal object, it does not view Him in the same proportion as He does Himself, totally, adequately, and with perfect penetration. This is why, strictly speaking, divine science and the beatific vision do not have a perfectly identical formal object, insofar as we are dealing with what is knowable and what is object (*absolute loquendo,*

*diviniae scientia et visionis beatificae formale objectum non
est prorsus idem in ratione congnoscibilis et objecti*). Thus
while intending to defend the Fathers against the charge of
error formulated by Vasquez, Ruiz adopts a method contrary to that of Suarez: instead of interpreting the texts
from the Fathers in the scholastic sense, he seeks to refor-
mulate the scholastic doctrine on divine incomprehensibility,
to the point that he falls into a kind of agnosticism: insofar as He is knowable, God is not a perfectly identical object
for Himself and for the created intellects enjoying the vision
of His essence.

These examples show all the difficulty of the problem
raised by Vasquez: the impossibility of interpreting the
Fathers properly and at the same time remaining within the
normal framework of scholastic thought. In this controversy
of the beginning of the seventeenth century, in the attempt
to reconcile the Fathers with the scholastics, doctrines which
neither professed were attached now to the former and now
to the latter.

This was well understood by Denis Petau, or Petavius
(1583-1652), the eminent Jesuit scholar.[5] He too resolutely
rejects the opinion of modern theologians (Ruiz) who wish
to see in comprehension a knowledge which would equal
the knowable nature of the object. If this were so one would
have to renounce not only the comprehension of God but also
the comprehension of created substances, for our knowledge is always accidental. The equality or commensurability
in knowledge, necessary if there is to be comprehension,
refers not to the essence of the object but to what is rep-
resentative of the object. Therefore the object of divine
comprehension and of created knowledge in the beatific
vision is perfectly identical, although this knowledge of the

---

[5]*De theologicis dogmatibus. De Deo Deique proprietatibus.* I. VII, vii:
*Deum in futura vita clare, et secundum essentiam videri primum ex antiquorom
Patrum auctoritate colligitur, tam graecorum quam latinorum; tum ex Scripto-
ris Graeci et Armeni contra sentientes refutati, et eorum firmamenta discussa.*
Ed. Bar-le-duc, 1864, Vol. I, pp. 571-6.

elect can never equal the amplitude of the object known (*amplitudinem rei cognitae*), i.e., can never comprehend the essence of God. It is in this sense that Petau would try to interpret the texts of the Fathers which deny the possibility of knowing God in His essence. However, in striving to reconcile the Fathers with scholastic doctrine, Petau takes good care not to do them violence, "to twist their necks," as he says, *obtorto quodammodo collo,* after the manner of his predecessors, which he feels is inadmissible for an honest and prudent theologian. Thus if he manages to uphold the honor of some of the Greek and Latin Fathers discredited by Vasquez, Petau experiences a certain embarrassment when he undertakes a scholastic interpretation of the homilies of St. John Chrysostom on the Incomprehensible. In the face of Greek and Syrian authors he renounces the whole attempt to interpret favorably the scholastic concept of the vision of God. Finally he enumerates some of those whose categorical statements are exactly contrary to the doctrine of the intuitive vision of the divine essence, including Titus of Bosrah, Theodoret of Cyrrhus, Theodore of Mopsuestia, Basil of Seleucia, Ecumenius, Anastasius the Sinaite, Theophylact of Bulgaria, and others.

Here Petau makes a very important remark which will determine the attitude of western scholars *vis-à-vis* Byzantine theologians in the question of the vision of God. In putting aside the ancient authors who denied, either in a confused way or in a more obvious manner (*obscure, vel evidentius*), the intuitive vision of the divine nature accessible to the blessed, Petau draws attention to more recent theologians who have professed the same doctrine, especially among the Greeks and Armenians.

He refers to Richard Radulph, or Fitzralph, the first western witness to this Eastern doctrine. Richard Fitzralph, Archbishop of Armagh, Primate of Ireland, charged by Pope Benedict XII to examine the doctrines of the Armenians seeking union with the Church of Rome in 1341, in his treatise

De quaestionibus Armenorum, I. xiv, ch. 1, actually blames the Armenians and the Greeks for having denied the vision of the divine essence. For Petau there is no doubt that the true authors of this error are to be sought among the Greeks. "Among the Greeks," he says, "the most tenacious defender of this opinion, the coryphaeus of this new faction, was Gregory Palamas, whose history and ridiculous doctrines (*ridicula dogmata*) we have traced in the first volume of our work" (in which Petau deals with the question of the attributes of God).

We should note that it is hardly possible that the Armenians to whom he refers in his study of Richard Fitzralph were influenced by Palamas. The theological controversy in Byzantium on the subject of the vision of God began only in 1339, and the first council to be called "Palamite" took place in 1341, at the very moment when the doctrinal points of the Armenians were being censured at Avignon by Benedict XII. However, as far as the beatific vision is concerned, Richard Fitzralph is thinking not so much about the opinions of the Armenians as the doctrines of the Byzantine theologians of his own time. In fact, in his *Summa in quaestionibus Armenorum,* I. xiv, devoted to the vision of God, he deals with "the modern Greek doctors and also certain of the Armenians" (*grecorum doctores moderni et etiam armenorum aliqui*).

Denis Petau was right to a certain extent: it is exactly in the fourteenth century, about the time of Gregory Palamas, that the contradiction between Byzantine theology and western scholasticism on the subject of the vision of God becomes manifest. But did he have the right to affirm, with the critics who follow in his tracks, that St. Gregory Palamas was an innovator, that the fourteenth century marks a rupture of tradition, at Byzantium, in the doctrines concerning the vision of God? As we have seen in our examination of the controversy raised by Gabriel Vasquez on the subject of the Greek Fathers, the efforts to reconcile the Fathers with the scholastics on the point which interests us raised some very delicate problems (the interpretation of *comprehensio*), occasioning a variety of attitudes, although the question posed by Vasquez could have been answered satisfactorily without them. Instead of resolving the difficulty of the Fathers, Denis Petau simply displaced it, directing attention elsewhere. Too prudent to strain the texts of the ancient writers by an interpretation to suit his own thesis, this scholar attacked more recent Byzantine theologians, making St. Gregory Palamas a target for all the charges Vasquez had formulated against the Fathers.

Among other things Petau reproaches the Byzantine theologians of the fourteenth century for having professed a doctrine of light uncreated yet visible to corporeal eyes, of splendor emanating from God, such as the apostles contemplated on Mount Tabor, the vision of which procures supreme beatitude for the elect in heaven, the very essence of God in itself, inaccessible to all knowledge. He quotes the words of the monk David who writes, in his history of the debate between Barlaam and Palamas: "All the saints, both men and angels, see the eternal glory of God and receive the gift and eternal grace; as for the substance of God, no one, neither men nor angels, sees it or is able to see it." Petau considers this doctrine "a senseless and barbarous fable" and bequeathes his indignation to all those in the West who, following him, deal with Byzantine theology of the fourteenth century. But indignation is not the way to study the history of religious ideas. Instead of seeking to understand how the question of the beatific vision is posed in the whole eastern tradition, modern critics attack the Byzantine theology of the fourteenth century exclusively, and, persuaded in advance that St. Gregory Palamas was an innovator, they wish to see his doctrine as an absurd invention, only because it is foreign to the principles formed by Latin scholasticism. Some modern polemicists, like Father Jugie and others, far from clearing the field of research done on the vision of God in Byzantine theology, complicate this purely doctrinal question in advance by attaching to it other problems of a spiritual and ascetic order, concerning the practice of mental prayer among Hesychast monks. No matter how interesting the spirituality of the Hesychasts may be, a study of this spirituality will not help us very much in clarifying the question of the vision of God in Byzantine theology. On the contrary, a study of doctrinal history can help us understand and judge better the spiritual life of the Hesychasts, and also Byzantine spirituality in general.

If we have spent some time on the controversy raised by Vasquez, it has been precisely in order to show that the question of the vision of God, not only among Byzantine theologians of the fourteenth century but also in earlier history, especially among the Greek Fathers, presents serious difficulties for those who want to study it from the standpoint of concepts appropriate to Latin scholasticism.

We do not claim to be making a reply to the question raised by Vasquez. We will simply try to see how the question of the vision of God is posed for the theologians of Byzantium, and, since the Byzantine theological tradition continues to develop the teachings of the Greek Fathers of the early Christian centuries, we must begin our studies with a rapid survey of their doctrines concerning the vision of God.

CHAPTER TWO

The Vision of God According to the Thought of the Bible and the Early Fathers

Byzantine theologians, especially the theologians of the fourteenth century, base their doctrine of the vision of God on two series of scriptural texts which seem contradictory and mutually exclusive. Indeed, alongside passages from Holy Scripture in which there can be found a formal negation of any vision of God, who is invisible, unknowable, inaccessible to created beings, there are others which encourage us to seek the face of God and promise the vision of God as He is, evidently representing this vision as the ultimate felicity of man.

Although Byzantine theologians of more recent times seem to have been struck especially by the contradictory way in which the vision of God is presented in Holy Scripture, other Christian thinkers have also sought to resolve this difficulty long before them, from the earliest ages of the Church. Together with their doctrine of the vision of God, Byzantine theologians also receive from their Greek and Syrian predecessors the manner of grouping the scriptural texts and of complementing them one with another. In the course of our studies we shall have to return constantly to these passages of Scripture, and it is for this reason that we must pause for a moment on certain texts from the Old and

New Testament which speak of the vision of God.

Among the texts which speak negatively of the vision of God we must cite first of all the passage from Exodus (33: 20-23) where God says to Moses: "You cannot see my Face, for man cannot see me and remain alive." God makes His glory pass by while He covers Moses with His hand, and Moses stands in a cleft of rock; when God raises His hand, Moses sees Him from the rear, without having been able to see His face. There are also other passages in the Old Testament (Judges 6: 22; 13: 22; Isa. 6: 5, etc.) which affirm that one cannot see God and remain alive. When God descends on Mount Sinai in a thick cloud, in the midst of fire, the people must remain apart that they may not die (Exod. 19: 21). Elijah wraps his face in his mantle when God appears to him (1 Kings 19: 13).

The cloud (γνόφος) in Psalm 97: 2[1] has the same meaning. It also expresses the inaccessible nature of God, the *tremendum*.[2] But at the same time this cloud points to the presence of God.[3] The pillar of cloud and of fire which goes before the Jews as they leave Egypt reveals God's presence at the same time that it conceals Him.[4]

New Testament texts are even more categorical in the negative sense. Thus St. Paul says (1 Tim. 6: 16): "God alone possesses immortality (ἀθανασίαν). He lives in unapproachable (ἀπρόσιτον) light; no man has seen him or can see him" (ὃν εἶδεν οὐδεὶς ἀνθρώπων οὐδὲ ἰδεῖν δύναται). Here the idea of immortality seems to have been attached to that of God's unknowable nature: He is inaccessible to a mortal being. St. John says (1 John 4: 12): "No one has ever seen God." (θεὸν οὐδεὶς πώποτε τεθέαται). Almost the same expression is found in the Gospel according to St. John (1: 18): θεὸν οὐδεὶς ἑώρακεν πώ-

[1] cf. Job 3: 5; 36: 29; 37: 16.
[2] cf. Ps. 36: 6; 57: 11; 108: 4; Isa. 14: 14; Job 21: 6; Ecclus. 35: 17ff.
[3] cf. Num. 12: 5; Ps. 99: 7; 104: 3; Isa. 19:1; Nah. 1: 3; Deut. 33: 26; Exod. 16: 10; 19: 9; Lev. 16: 2; Job 22: 11; Dan. 7: 13; 2 Macc. 2: 8; etc.
[4] cf. Exod. 13: 21; 14: 19; Deut. 31: 15; Neh. 9: 12; Wis. 19: 7.

ποτε, but here St. John adds: "The only begotten Son,[5] who is in the bosom of the Father, he (ἐκεῖνος) has manifested (or rather explained, interpreted: ἐξηγήσατο) him." It is the property of the Word (Λόγος) to express, to tell the nature of the Father. And further on (John 6: 46): "No one has seen the Father, except him who is with God (παρὰ τοῦ θεοῦ); he has seen the Father." The same idea is expressed in the synoptic gospels (Matthew 11: 27 and Luke 10: 22): "No one knows (ἐπιγινώσκει) the Son, except the Father, and no one knows the Father except the Son and him to whom the Son chooses to reveal (ἀποκαλύψαι) him." While they limit the vision and knowledge of God to the intimate relationship of the Father and the Son who alone know one another, these last texts (from St. John and the synoptics) also affirm that such knowledge can be conferred on or communicated to created beings by the will of the Son.

Here we are brought face to face with a series of many texts which affirm the possibility of seeing God. There is not sufficient space to enumerate here all the "theophanies" or appearances of God in the Old Testament. There is the often mentioned appearance of an angel, a kind of proxy by means of which God assumes the form of a man (Gen. 16: 7-14, etc.). Isaiah calls him the "Angel of presence" (63: 9). God remains unknown, but His personal presence is made known, as in the episode where Jacob wrestles with God (Gen. 32: 24-30). The Unknown One refuses to reveal His name, but Jacob says: "I have seen God face to face, and yet my soul is still alive." And he calls the place where God appeared to him "Penuel," which means "the face of God." God speaks to Moses "face to face," as one speaks to a friend (Exod. 33: 11; Deut. 34: 10). It is a personal meeting with a personal God, even though on Mount Sinai He is enveloped in mystery and darkness.[6] Moses' face shines

[5]Or, according to another reading, "The only begotten God (μονογενὴς θεός)."

[6]cf. Exod. 19: 9-25; 24: 9-18; 33: 11-23; 34: 4-8; Deut. 5: 4.

from the reflection of the face of God (Exod. 34: 29), for
the face of God is luminous. "Let thy face shine upon us,
O Lord" (Num. 6: 25); and the Psalms speak of "the light
of God's face."[7] I leave aside the numerous texts in the Old
Testament concerning the glory (*kabod*, or in the Septuagint:
δόξα), which both reveals and dissimulates the presence of
God, that we may come to the Book of Job, where the
righteous one tried by God expresses not only a hope in
the resurrection but also confidence that he will see God
with his own eyes (Job 19: 25-27): "I know that my Redeemer
lives and that at the last day he will restore this skin which
is falling into corruption, and in my flesh I shall see God.
I shall see him for myself, my own eyes and not those of
another will see him." And further on (42: 5): "I have
heard thee by the hearing of my ear but now, in this place,
my eyes behold thee."

If in the Old Testament the person of God is often
represented by an angel (Isaiah's "Angel of presence," who
reveals the presence of God), we find just the opposite in
the New Testament: it is the angels of human persons who
"always behold the face of their heavenly Father" (Matthew
18: 10). As the Epistle to the Hebrews puts it (chaps. 1
and 2), it is not by angels but by His Son that God speaks
now to men. If in the Old Testament men with clean hands
and pure hearts are called "the generation of those who seek
the face of the God of Jacob" (Ps. 24: 4-6), the Gospel
asserts that the "pure in heart" will see God (Matthew 5:
8). In speaking of the elect the Apocalypse says: "and they
will see his face and his name will be on their foreheads"
(22: 4).

The texts of the New Testament are of the first im-
portance in the question of the vision of God. These are the
First Epistle of St. John 3: 1-2 and the First Epistle of St.
Paul to the Corinthians 13: 12. For St. John the vision of
God is connected with the quality of being a son of God,

[7]Ps. 4: 6; 31: 16; 67: 1; 80: 3, 19; 90: 8.

a quality conferred on Christians by the love (ἀγάπη) of the Father. The world, he says, does not know us (as sons of God) because it has not known God. But we are already, from this moment on, sons of God (τέκνα θεοῦ) and what we shall be has not yet appeared (καὶ οὔπω ἐφανερώθη τί ἐσόμεθα), i.e., the fruit of this adoption—its final realization—is not yet manifested. We know that when He appears we shall be like Him, for we shall see Him as He is (ὅμοιοι αὐτῷ ἐσόμεθα, ὅτι ὀψόμεθα αὐτὸν καθώς ἐστιν). We already see what doctrinal riches are contained implicitly in these two verses. In effect, the text which we have just quoted relates the vision of God first of all to the adoption of Christians who are called the "sons" or "children" of God; it then relates it to Christian eschatology, the manifestation of our final state or indeed the final manifestation of God, in the parousia, for the words ἐὰν φανερωθῆ, "when he [it] will appear," can be translated in these two ways; the text also establishes a relationship between the vision of God and the deified state of the elect who become "likenesses of God" (ὅμοιοι αὐτῷ); it alludes to the divine charity or love (ἀγάπη) which confers on Christians the quality of being sons of God, with all that this involves. The different interpretations which may be given to this text from St. John can be foreseen already. Thus, "we shall be like him, for we shall see him as he is" can be interpreted in the sense of a causal relationship: the deified state is the consequence of the vision of God as He is. Or, the ὅτι ὀψόμεθα, "for we shall see him," may be given a demonstrative meaning ("we shall be likeness of him, since we shall see him"): the fact that we see God as He is shows that we are likenesses of Him. In the same way καθώς ἐστιν will be rich in meaning for theological thought.

The text from St. Paul is no less important for the theology of vision. In chapter 13 of the First Epistle to the Corinthians, St. Paul intends to show the "excellent way"

which surpasses all others—ὑπερβολὴν ὁδόν, that most
perfect gift which we must seek—the gift of ἀγάπη. After
his celebrated hymn to ἀγάπη, St. Paul declares that this
alone will never cease, while all other gifts—the gifts of
prophecy, tongues, knowledge (γνῶσις) will be abolished.
"For we know in part (ἐκ μέρους) and prophesy in part.
But when the perfect (τὸ τέλειον) comes, that which is in
part (τὸ ἐκ μέρους) will be done away. In the same way
when one becomes a man (the perfect state), the manner of
speaking and feeling proper for children will be abolished."
Then he opposes the imperfect or partial (τὸ ἐκ μέρους),
to the perfect (τὸ τέλειον), or final state to which man is
called. "Now we see as in a mirror, darkly—βλέπομεν γὰρ
ἄρτι δι' ἐσόπτρου ἐν αἰνίγματι, then we shall see face
to face—τότε δὲ πρόσωπον πρὸς πρόσωπον." The partial
vision "in a mirror" (δι' ἐσόπτρου) can signify God's
manifestation in His creation, accessible even to the Gentiles,
that "invisible nature of God" which can be perceived by
contemplating created things (Rom. 1: 19-20). The perfect,
immediate "face to face" vision is opposed here to the imperfect, partial vision of God. Boussuet notes that any one
who sees an object in a mirror does not have it "face to
face" but has his back to it; one must therefore turn one's
back to the mirror in order to see the object itself. This
interpretation is ingenious, but it must not be forgotten that
in speaking of the face to face vision of God, St. Paul is
repeating the familiar expression of the Bible in which
"face to face" denotes a meeting with a God-Person. In
the phrase that follows the perfect nature of this knowledge of God is qualified very precisely: "Now I know in
part, but then I shall know as I have been known"—or "to
the extent that I have been known." If we forget that a
few verses before the γνῶσις had to yield precedence to
ἀγάπη in the perfect state of the age to come, knowledge
of God will be made the supreme end of man. Then, with
an intellectual emphasis, this text will be interpreted in the

sense of an equality of knowledge: "I shall know God to the same extent that he knows me." But if on the contrary the idea of ἀγάπη is kept in mind, to which the whole chapter is devoted, then this passage concerning reciprocity of knowledge will be related to another text from the same Epistle (1 Cor. 8: 2-3) where St. Paul says: "If anyone thinks he posseses knowledge of something, he has not yet known in the way he ought to know; but if anyone loves God, he is known by him. Εἰ δέ τις ἀγαπᾷ τὸν θεόν, οὗτος ἔγνωσται ὑπ᾽ αὐτοῦ." An object is known; this is an imperfect knowledge in which there is no reciprocity; where there is reciprocity of knowledge, knowledge signifies a relationship between persons, it is determined by ἀγάπη. To see God face to face is to know Him as He knows us, just as two friends know one another reciprocally. Such a knowledge-vision, presupposing reciprocity, excludes all idea of finality in the face to face vision of God. It is not the final cause determining love but an expression of that ἀγάπη which awaits its perfection (τὸ τέλειον) in the age to come.

The scriptural texts touching on the vision of God which we have just looked over will help us judge in what measure the theology of the Fathers, especially Byzantine theology, has remained pure of all accretion alien to the Christian tradition while developing this original data. If, as we have seen in the first chapter, Gabriel Vasquez in the sixteenth century criticized those Fathers whose doctrines did not correspond to the scholastic ideas of an intuitive vision of the divine essence, a Protestant theologian in our own time, Anders Nygren, directs a reproach against the Fathers of the Church and the whole Eastern theological tradition which is quite contrary to the reproach of Vasquez. In his thought-provoking book published in French under the title *Eros et agapé*, Nygren opposes the purely Christian notion of agape, a wholly gratuitous love which is, according to Nygren, exclusively the way of God toward man, to the pagan notion of eros, a calculating and egotistic love, drawing man toward God and provoking in him the desire for joy, a way which is exclusively that of man toward God. "Vision," says Nygren, "is therefore the principal response caused by eros. Without doubt the idea of the vision of God is encountered also in agape, but in a totally different sense."[8] Over the course of the history of Christian thought a compromise has been made between the agape of St. Paul and the eros of Hellenistic philosophy. "Eros," writes Nygren, "is developed along a continuous line which begins with neo-platonism and the theology of Alexandria, passes through Dionysius the Areopagite and partially through Augustine, Erigena and the mysticism of the Middle Ages, and ends with German idealism and the post-Kantian speculative systems."[9] The result of this compromise with Platonism, as far as it concerns the vision of God, is that the "mystical contemplation of God, one of the salient characteristics of religion founded on eros, has from the beginning been connected with the word: Blessed are the pure in heart, for they will see God. It has not been noticed that there is an abyss between the eschatological vision of God, which is what we are studying here, and the mystical contemplation of God, nor that the former is only a way of expressing the perfect realization of communion with God."[10] Both Vasquez and Nygren criticize the Fathers: the former in the name of scholasticism and the latter in the name of revealed religion. The former insists especially on man's ascent to God and reproaches the majority of the Greek Fathers for not having made God an object of knowledge; Nygren on the contrary seems to bear a grudge against them because they have substituted the contemplation of God for His eschatological manifestation. To what extent are these contradictory reproaches applicable to Byzantine theology? This is what we shall try to see by at-

[8]p. 250.
[9]p. 247.
[10]pp. 255-6.

tempting first to define the place which the vision of God has held among Christian authors in the East prior to Byzantine theology properly so called.

* * *

We shall concentrate first on two Christian authors of the second century: St. Theophilus of Antioch and St. Irenaeus.

The only work of Theophilus which has come down to us in full is an apology in three books addressed to an educated pagan called Autolycus. It must have been written between 178 and 182. In Book I chapters 1 to 17,[11] Theophilus deals with the question of the possibility of seeing God.

Autolycus, who extols the cult of idols, asks Theophilus to show him the God of the Christians. Theophilus answers him: "Before I show you our God, show me your man; give me proof that the eyes of your soul can see and the ears of your heart hear. For only those who have the eyes of their soul open can see God. On the contrary those whose eyes are obscured (ὑποκεχυμένους) by the cataracts of sin cannot see God. Can God be described to those who cannot see Him? His form (εἶδος) is unspeakable, inexpressible, since it is invisible to carnal eyes. If I say that it is light, I am speaking of something which is produced (ποίημα). If I call him the Word (Λόγος), I am speaking of his principle (ἀρχή)." Undoubtedly this is a reference to the principle of His manifestation. The terms used here by St. Theophilus are rather vague and we dare not define them too clearly, we must avoid distorting his thought by interpreting these expressions in the precise sense they have in the theology of a later age. Thus the word ποίημα as applied to φῶς—does it mean "created" (it would refer then to created light, a concept which is then applied to God by analogy); or does it actually mean "produce," the

[11]PG. 6, cols. 1024-36.

way in which God is manifested as light? It is difficult to decide with any assurance.

"If I call him Intelligence (νοῦς), I am speaking of his prudence (φρόνησις). If I call him Spirit (πνεῦμα), this refers to his breath. If I call him Wisdom (σοφία), it is of his offspring that I am speaking. The name Power (δύναμις) denotes his energy. When I call him Providence (πρόνοια), this refers to his goodness. Kingdom denotes his glory. The name of Lord is applied to his nature as Judge, and the name Judge denotes the justice which he represents. If I call him Father I am saying that he is everything [undoubtedly in the sense of the universal cause of being]. Finally, when I say that he is Fire, I signify by this term his wrath. ... Everything has been created from nothing (ἐξ οὐκ ὄντων εἰς τὸ εἶναι), so that the majesty of God (τὸ μέγεθος αὐτοῦ) might be known and grasped by the mind through his works." The divine names enumerated here by Theophilus relate therefore to the majesty of God appearing in creation, "like the human soul which, while it remains invisible, makes itself known by the movements of the body which it animates. Thus God, who created all things by the Word and by Wisdom, can be known in his providence and in his works (διὰ τῆς προνοίας καὶ τῶν ἔργων)." This is a development of the Epistle to the Romans ("the invisible nature of God becomes visible in creation"), a development which makes us think of the πρόνοιαι ἐκφαντορικαί of Dionysius, with his method of forming the divine names from the acts of providence while borrowing them from Holy Scripture.

This is not yet a direct vision, even though God who has created all things by the Word and by Wisdom already appears as a Trinity: the unknown Father manifesting Himself in the world by the Son and the Holy Spirit.

For Autolycus to know God it is necessary that God open his eyes, like a doctor who removes the cataracts (is this an allusion to baptism, illumination?). Faith in and fear of God are necessary conditions for understanding that God established the earth by His Wisdom and formed the heavens in His loving care. If having understood that, Autolycus were then to live a life of justice and purity, he would be able to see God. But this vision will take place only after the resurrection. "When you have disposed of your corruptible nature (τὸ θνητὸν) and are clothed in incorruptibility (ἀφθαρσία), you will see God, in so far as you are worthy (κατ' ἀξίαν). For God will revive your flesh (by making it) immortal with the soul, and then, having become immortal, you will see the Immortal One, if you have believed in him now."

The eschatological vision of God will become accessible to mortal beings when they are clothed in incorruptibility. A reply can be seen here to St. Paul's negative text: "God alone possesses immortality; he lives in unapproachable light; no man has seen him nor can see him" (1 Tim. 6: 16); and to all the passages of Scripture which assert that we cannot see God face to face and remain alive. The vision of God about which Theophilus of Antioch is speaking here is attributed to the human being in his totality: soul and body become immortal after the resurrection. This is a communion of men (clothed in incorruptibility) with God (who is incorruptible by nature) in which no distinction between intellectual knowledge and sense perception impedes the act of vision. This is not so much a contemplation of God as a final manifestation in which God will appear to each man to the extent that he has become worthy of seeing Him. The eschatological character of the early Christian centuries, the waiting for the perfect revelation of God after the consummation of the age, can be sensed in this thought, which draws its substance from the Holy Scriptures.

*   *   *

The same eschatological concept of the vision of God,

as the final manifestation of that for which humanity has been progressively prepared, the same relating of this face to face vision with the state of incorruptibility, appears in St. Irenaeus of Lyon (died. *c.* 202). His principal work: *Against Heresies, False Gnosis Unmasked and Refuted* (in which he opposes the tradition of the Church to the gnostic doctrines) was written between 180 and 190. The Greek text has come down to us in several fragments. The rest of it is known to us in a Latin translation which must be very ancient, perhaps contemporary to St. Irenaeus, since Tertullian already quotes it just twenty years after Irenaeus' death.

Struggling against the gnostic theories which were seeking to oppose a creating god, a demiurge, to the saving God who had appeared in Jesus Christ, Irenaeus develops the idea of a progressive revelation of God who creates all things by the Word, a revelation which the Word continues by manifesting Himself to the patriarchs and prophets, and which He consummates in the Incarnation. The Word denotes here the actual principle of the revelation of the Father, to which is applied the idea of God invisible by nature. Unknowable in His majesty, God makes Himself known in His love by the Word, by whom He has created all things.[12] "It is the Son who in manifesting himself gives knowledge of the Father; for knowledge of the Father is the manifestation of the Son." A little further on St. Irenaeus adds: "The Father is the invisible nature of the Son, while the Son is the visible nature of the Father."[13]

"The Word is manifested when he is made man. Before the Incarnation it was right to say that man had been made in the image of God, but it could not be demonstrated, for the Word—the One in whose image man had been made—was still invisible. Moreover, the likeness itself had been quickly lost. The Word-become-flesh restored his image and

[12]*Against Heresies* IV 20, 4. PG. 7, col. 1034.
[13]*Against Heresies* IV 6, 3-6, col. 988.

likeness, for he himself became what was made in his image, and he expressed the likeness profoundly by making man similar, through the visible Word, to the invisible Father."[14] It is through the Holy Spirit that man acquires this likeness. "If in a man the Spirit is not united to the soul, this man is imperfect; he remains animal and carnal; he does have the image of God in his flesh, but he is not receiving the likeness through the Spirit."[15] Thus the economy of the Son and the Holy Spirit "raises man to the life of God."[16] The progressive manifestation of God is accomplished now in the spiritual progress of man, realizing his likeness received in the promise of the Spirit. This ascending path toward the state of the spiritual man transcends the distinctions so dear to the gnostics—of somatic, psychic and pneumatic man. A new scriptural element now begins to enrich the doctrine of the knowledge of God: i.e. the quality of man created in the image and likeness of God; a quality which is realized fully both by the fact of the Incarnation (the Son being manifested as the perfect image of the invisible Father, in whose image man has been created), and by the promised descent of the Holy Spirit, conferring on man the possibility of progress, of spiritual life. This spiritual progress of man, being raised by the Spirit and the Word to communion with the Father, receives an eschatological emphasis in St. Irenaeus' writing: "If now," he says, "having received the promise of the Spirit, we cry: Abba Father, what will it be like when, after we are resurrected, we see him face to face—when all the members, coming together in a great throng, chant the hymn of triumph in honor of him who resurrected them from death and endowed them with life eternal?"[17]

The vision of God for St. Irenaeus is always a revelation accomplished by the will of God. God is not by nature an object that can be known, but He makes Himself known. He

[14]ibid., V 16, 2, cols. 1167-8.
[15]ibid., V 6, 1, cols. 1137-8.
[16]ibid., V 9, 1, col. 1144
[17]ibid., V 8, 1, col. 1141.

reveals Himself out of love, out of condescension. If the
prophets have announced that men will see God, if the
Lord has promised this vision to the pure in heart, it is
just as true that "no one will see God." Indeed when we
consider His grandeur and His glory, no one is able to see
God without dying; for the Father is beyond perception
(*incapabilis*); but by virtue of His charity, His love for
men, and His all-powerfulness (*secundum autem dilectionem
et humanitatem et quod omnia possit*), He bestows this great
gift on those who love Him, this vision of God, just as the
prophets proclaimed, since what is impossible for man is
possible for God. Actually "man himself does not see God,
but God, because He wills it, is seen by men, by those whom
He chooses, when He chooses and as He chooses."[18] A latent
distinction is glimpsed here between two aspects of God—
secundum magnitudinem et secundum dilectionem. This
would suggest that God, though inaccessible by nature, reveals Himself by grace. But we must not strain the text.
For St. Irenaeus, whose trinitarian terminology is different
from that which will become the classic doctrine of the
Trinity in the fourth century, the notion of the nature of
God in Himself is connected with the name of Father, while
the name Word is applied to His external manifestation.
However, the existence of the Word is not apparently subordinated in his thought to God's will to create or manifest
Himself. The Son is the natural manifestation of God, He is
"the visible nature of the Father," as the Father is "the invisible
nature of the Son." If will intervenes, it is to bestow the
vision of God on those whom He chooses—*per Sanctus
Spiritus beneplacitum*—by the good will of the Holy Spirit.

St. Irenaeus distinguishes three degrees of vision: the
prophetic vision through the Holy Spirit, the vision of
adoption through the Son, and the vision of the Father in
the Kingdom of heaven. The Spirit prepares man in the Son
of God, the Son brings him to the Father, the Father con-

18ibid., IV 20, 5, col. 1035.

fers on him the incorruptibility of eternal life, that man might understand from the fact itself that he sees God."[19] This passage is extremely rich in doctrinal ideas, which St. Irenaeus develops elsewhere. The first thing that strikes us here is that the vision of God in the Kingdom of heaven communicates eternal life by rendering man incorruptible. The face of God which one could not see without dying becomes in the age to come the source of life. "For men," says St. Irenaeus, "will see God in order to live, having become immortal by the vision and progressing now on the way to God" (*per visionem immortales facti et peregrinantes usque in Deum*). Just before this he remarks, in a passage which has come down to us in the original text: "It is impossible to live without life. Now the existence (ὕπαρξις) of life proceeds from participation (μετοχή) in God. But to participate in God is to know (γιγνώσκειν) him (the Latin text says *videre*, to see) and to enjoy his goodness."[20] It is not just a question here of eternal life, of the incorruptibility which is received by way of vision in the age to come—by perfect participation in the divine life—but rather of life in general, which is also a kind of participation and therefore a partial vision of God. This need not surprise us, since creation already is represented, for St. Irenaeus, as a manifestation of God, and He who manifests Himself becomes apparent, shows Himself. The invisible God manifests Himself, shows Himself by the Word, the principle of all manifestation. Actually the Word shows God to men at the same time that He shows or exhibits (*exhibet*) man to God. We recognize here the reciprocity of vision asserted by St. Paul. But the passage from St. Irenaeus which we are now studying[21] does not refer to the perfect, face to face vision; it refers to the manifestation of God by the Word before His incarnation. This is a vision of God which St.

[19]ibid., IV 20, 3, col. 1035.
[20]ibid., III 20, 5, cols. 1035-6.
[21]ibid., V 20, 7, col. 1037.

Irenaeus calls elsewhere[22] a "figurative participation" in incorruptibility, in the perfect life. This perfect life will not appear, will not become visible until after the Incarnation, which will render men capable of taking full part in life, in incorruptibility. As we have said, it is the vision of the Father which makes us incorruptible. Before the Incarnation the Word, while manifesting God in creation, safeguards the invisibility of the Father so that man, being insufficiently prepared for such intimacy, will not begin to despise God. But at the same time the Word by no means leaves God totally hidden from man: He reveals Him in several dispositions (*per multas dispositiones*, undoubtedly we must read this as *dispensationes*—economies), which correspond to the figurative or prophetic visions of God. The revelatory economy is indispensable "so that man, in completely turning away from God, will not cease to exist" (*ne in totum deficiens a Deo homo, cessaret esse*). We see here the rough draft of an ontology which St. Irenaeus does not develop: the existence of created being depends on a participation in God, a participation which is effected by a certain kind of vision. St. Irenaeus continues: "For the glory of God is a living man, while the life of man is the vision of God. Therefore if the manifestation of God in creation *per conditionem* already confers life to all that dwells on earth, so much the more does the manifestation of the Father by the Word communicate life to those who see God."[23] This brings us again to the three degrees of vision pointed out by St. Irenaeus: the prophetic vision in the Holy Spirit, the vision of adoption in the Incarnate Son, the vision of the Father in the age to come. These three stages, as we shall see, fit together in such a way that each one is virtually contained in the other. St. Irenaeus stresses the fact that the prophets did not clearly see the actual face of God, but that it ap-

[22]In his *Treatise on the Apostolic Preaching*, Armenian text, Eastern Fathers, Vol. 12, p. 771, art. 31.
[23]*Against Heresies* IV, 20, 7, col. 1037.

peared to them in the mysterious economy by which men
were beginning to see God.[24] They could see only "the likenesses of the splendor of the Lord" (*similitudines claritatis
Domini*), a preview of the future manifestation. While the
Father remained invisible the Word showed the splendor
of the Father within the limits of the way He had chosen
to make this manifestation. This is the figurative or prophetic
vision, attributed here not to the economy of the Holy Spirit
but to the economy of the Word, for together and in-
separably the Word and the Holy Spirit constitute the principle of manifestation. This vision of "the likenesses of the
splendor of the Father" already contains the premises for the
perfect vision which will be realized later. God appeared to
Moses on Mount Sinai *in conspectu*—"in presence," as to a
friend. It was actually the Word who appeared to him; but
Moses could not see Him and begged for a clear vision of
the One who was speaking to him. Clinging to a rocky crag,
Moses then received a figurative vision of God—*videbis quae
sunt posteriora mea*. This means two things for St. Irenaeus:
first, that it is impossible for man to see God; and second,
that man will see God later, *in novissimis temporibus*, on
the summit of the rocky crag, i.e. in His human Coming (*in
eo qui est secundum hominem ejus adventu*), in the Incarnate
Word. "This is why," he says, "Moses conversed with God
face to face on the summit of a mountain, accompanied by
Elijah, as the Gospel tells us, so that at the end God carried
out the promise he made at the beginning."[25] The vision on
Mount Sinai finds its fulfilment, its plenitude realized at
last on Mount Tabor, where Moses and Elijah (who had
also, like him, received a figurative vision of God) appeared
on either side of the transfigured Christ. Thus the prophetic
vision was already a participation in the final state, in the
incorruptibility of the age to come revealed in Christ's transfiguration, in the "Kingdom of God coming in power."

[24]ibid., IV 20, 10, col. 1038.
[25]ibid., IV 20, 9, col. 1038.

For St. Irenaeus the third stage, the vision of the Father, the vision possessed by the blessed, is expressed in the appearance of Christ transfigured by that light which is the source of the incorruptible life of the age to come. He is saying, in effect: "The Word was made flesh . . . so that all that exists could see . . . its King; and also that the light of the Father might fill the body of our Lord and, through his body, come to us; so that man might arrive at incorruptibility, being clothed in the light of the Father."[26]

The theme of Christ's transfiguration reappears constantly in the writings of the Byzantine theologians; it will be the keystone of their doctrines of the vision of God. In St. Irenaeus this theme appears for the first time, so far as I know, in a doctrinal context which connects it with the vision of the age to come: the vision of Christ in His glory, the vision by which man participates in the light of the Invisible God, receiving in this way the state of incorruptibility or deification. For "if the Word is made man, it is that men might become gods,"[27] St. Irenaeus says, and his words will be repeated by the Fathers and theologians from age to age. Now what is the deification of created beings, if not their perfect participation in the divine life? This participation is expressed best by the concept of light. "To see the light," says St. Irenaeus, "is to be in the light and to participate in its clarity; in the same way, to see God is to be in him and to participate in his life-giving splendor. Therefore those who see God participate in life."[28]

Beatitude is for St. Irenaeus an infinite progress in man and an increasing manifestation of God. "Even in the world to come," he says, "God will always have to instruct and man will always have to learn from God."[29]

St. Irenaeus has often been reproached for having professed millenarianism, the doctrine of the millenial reign of

[26]ibid., IV 20, 2, col. 1033.
[27]ibid., V pref., col. 1035.
[28]ibid., IV 2, 5, col. 1035.
[29]ibid., II 28, 2-3, col. 805.

the righteous which, according to the Apocalypse, will be realized on earth before the end of the world. He does speak of the "mystery of resurrection and the reign of the righteous, the beginning of incorruptibility, a reign in which those who are worthy will be accustomed little by little to the knowledge of God" (*Paulatim assuescunt capere Deum*).[30] And later he adds: "The righteous will reign on earth, increasing in the vision of the Lord, and in this way they will become accustomed to receive the glory of God the Father."[31] This is quite in line with St. Irenaeus' thought: i.e. if the deifying light of the Father appeared on earth in the transfigured Christ, then the vision of the Father appropriate to the age to come can begin here too. For an author writing in the age of early Christianity this participation (in a final incorruptibility made possible on earth) will appear in the eschatological perspective of the Apocalypse, as the mysterious state of the righteous, resurrected to enjoy communion with God on earth. But the state of perfect beatitude is reserved for heaven. Sketching a picture of the new heaven and the new earth, St. Irenaeus tells us: "Then, according to the word of our forefathers, those who are worthy of the celestial habitations will pass into heaven. Some will enjoy the delights of paradise (this undoubtedly refers to the earthly paradise). Others will finally possess the splendor of the City (the celestial Jerusalem descending from heaven). Nevertheless the Savior will be visible everywhere, to the extent that those who see him are worthy of such a vision."[32] By interpreting in this way the words of St. John's Gospel: "In my Father's house are many habitations," he develops the idea of a vision of God differing for each person.[33]

Such then is St. Irenaeus' doctrine of the vision of God. As with St. Theophilus of Antioch, the vision of God is connected with incorruptibility. But here it becomes the

[30] ibid., V 32, 1, col. 1210.
[31] ibid., V 35, 1, col. 1218.
[32] ibid., V 36, 1 col. 1222.
[33] ibid., V 36, 2, col. 1223.

source of eternal life and even the source of all existence, since vision means participation. By vision we participate in God, just as we participate in light by seeing it. Now the invisible God is revealed in Christ transfigured by the light of the Father, the light in which man receives the incorruptible state of eternal life. The possibility of enjoying this deifying vision here on earth by receiving the light of the Father through the Incarnate Word is, for St. Irenaeus, projected on to an eschatological plane—it signifies the millenial reign of the righteous. It would seem that the theme of mystical contemplation was not raised for him in any other way than a new historical epoch for mankind, in which the righteous will be gradually accustomed to perfect communion with God. We are going to see that this question of mystical contemplation is presented in a totally different light in the writings of Clement of Alexandria and Origen.

CHAPTER THREE

Alexandria

The millenarian or Chiliastic doctrines begin to disappear with the decline of the eschatological spirit which characterizes the first two Christian centuries. In the third century they will be fought vigorously, especially in Egypt, first by Origen and then by his disciple St. Dionysius of Alexandria. The reason why these yearnings for a future reign of the righteous who will live on earth in communion with God begin to lose their meaning is not to be sought just in the naïvely materialistic form which they had taken occasionally (in Papias, for example, who was criticized by Irenaeus), nor simply in the way Chiliasm was discredited by the extravagant pretensions of the Montanist sect. The increasing opposition to the doctrines of the advent of the new age marked by a new clear manifestation of God is only partially explained by the allegorical spirit of the new school of Christianity in Alexandria, which refused to attach itself to the Judaistic letter and sought a spiritual meaning in the sacred writings. If there is now a rejection of the idea of a new stage in communion with God in the form of a future reign of the righteous, it is because there is a wish to show that from now on the way to this degree of perfection is open to Christians in a spiritual life devoted to the contemplation of God. This ideal of the contemplative life will—at least at first—borrow forms which are all too reminiscent of Hellenistic wisdom, especially when contemplation is opposed to action as a state of perfection, as the Christian's ultimate goal.

The Protestant theologian Anders Nygren, to whom we have referred in the preceding chapter, wishes to see this fact as the result of a substitution of Christian *agape* by pagan *eros*. "It has not been noticed," he says, "that there is an abyss between the eschatological vision ... and the mystical contemplation of God, and that the first is the only way of expressing the perfect realization of Christian communion." Thus the whole of Christian mysticism appears to him as a deviation or Platonic distortion of primitive Christianity.

Fr. Festugière arrived independently at the same conclusions concerning the ideal of the contemplative life. In his article "Asceticism and Contemplation"[1] he writes as follows: "From the third century on another tradition can be seen running parallel to the specifically Christian tradition, in which what had come down from Jesus is merged with an element of pagan wisdom and is sometimes absorbed by it. The origin of this movement is quite clear: it is the Alexandrian school of Clement and Origen."[2] Fr. Festugière does not stop here. Like Nygren, although with more reserve, he wishes to see almost all subsequent speculative mysticism as the result of a synthesis or symbiosis between Athens and Jerusalem. "The links in the chain are readily discerned," he says, "they are all the teachers of contemplation in the East, Evagrius, Gregory of Nyssa, Diadochus of Photice, the Pseudo-Dionysius; in the West, Augustine and (to the extent that he follows Augustine) Gregory the Great."[3]

Later on, in our examination of the doctrine of the vision of God in Gregory of Nyssa, Diadochus and Dionysius, we shall try to see clearly how far we can accept Fr. Festugière's thesis concerning these writers. For the moment we shall limit

[1] *The Child of Agrigento,* Paris, 1941, pp. 131-46.
[2] ibid., p. 138.
[3] ibid.

ourselves to a brief examination of the vision of God in the writings of the two great masters of the Alexandrian Didascalion, Clement and Origen, whom Fr. Festugière regards as the founders of what he calls "philosophical spirituality." He defines it in this way: "It is an intellectualistic or super-intellectualistic mysticism, leading to a kind of exclusively contemplative life which leaves no room at all for action inspired by love." "Perfection is equated to contemplation, and to contemplate is to see God in an immediate vision."[4]

* * *

Clement of Alexandria was born *c.* 150; he taught until the year 203, when the persecution of Septimus Severus forced him to leave Alexandria. He died *c.* 215. His chief works are the *Protreptikos* or *Exhortation to the Greeks,* in which he addresses himself to those without, to the pagans; the *Paidagogos,* directed to catechumens or simple-minded believers in need of instruction; and the *Stromateis* or *Miscellanies,* a sort of mosaic formed of sometimes disparate pieces which seem to be the outlines for an instruction of more fully self-conscious Christians.

A certain esotericism appears in this concern to portion out instruction according to the hearer's degree of perfection, and Clement sometimes expresses himself in terms borrowed deliberately from the pagan mysteries. Thus he notes that the Greek mysteries begin with a purification, which finds its analogy in Christian confession. Then we are initiated to the "lesser mysteries" (μικρὰ μυστήρια), a kind of instruction or doctrinal preparation for the μεγάλα μυστήρια, the "greater mysteries," in which we no longer learn about the realities but contemplate them. This is the ἐποπτεία, for Christians the highest degree of initiation to the contemplation of God, arrived at by way of analysis. Clement

[4]ibid., p. 139.

gives us an example of this intellectual process which ends in contemplation.

Beginning with a body, we proceed by a series of abstractions which first of all suppress its physical qualities. There remains a certain extension (trans: *étendue*). By suppressing the dimensions of depth, size, length, we obtain a point occupying a certain place, the site of the point in space; we find ourselves confronted by a certain unity, an intelligible monad. If then we suppress all that can be attributed to beings, both corporeal and incorporeal, we are precipitated (ἀπορρίψομεν) into the majesty (μέγεθος) of Christ; if we pass on from there through sanctity towards the abyss (βάθος), we will have a particular knowledge of God, "who contains all" (παντοκράτωρ), in this way coming to know not what He is, but what He is not (οὐχ ὃ ἐστίν, ὃ δὲ μή ἐστιν γνωρίσαντες).[5]

This text from Clement, in which we see a kind of negative or apophatic way to the knowledge of God, reminds us of the analytical speculation which Plotinus will describe in the sixth Ennead, sixty years after Clement. For Plotinus the path of intellectual abstractions, of a simplification (ἅπλοσις) or reduction to the one, will end in a type of experience the ecstatic character of which will be even more pronounced than in the thought of his Christian predecessor. For Plotinus all knowledge will be suppressed in the ecstatic state, where there is no longer either subject or object but only the experience of perfect identity with the One. It would seem that Clement remains on the intellectual plane in proposing that God is to be known by what He is not, even though before arriving at this negative knowledge we must go beyond the intelligible monad, be thrown into contemplation of the majesty of Christ, in order to attain afterwards, "through sanctity," the abyss of the Father. This passage is not very clear. Let us leave it for the time being. One thing is certain: he is referring here to a contemplation

[5]*Stromateis* V, 11. PG. 9, cols. 101-8.

which we may consider (with Fr. Festugière) as belonging
to an intellectualistic or super-intellectualistic mysticism.

This contemplation has for its object God, who surpasses
the One, who is above unity (ἓν δὲ ὁ θεός, καὶ ἐπέκεινα
τοῦ ἑνός, καὶ ὑπὲρ αὐτὴν μονάδα).[6] All notions which
we can have of Him are "unformed" (ἀειδεῖς ἐννοίας).[7]
In fact it is impossible to apply to Him either type, or dif-
ferentiality, or species, or individuality, or any of the logical
categories. He is neither accidental, nor One to whom accidental qualities can be attributed; neither all, nor part. We
can say that He is infinite because He has no dimension. He
is without form, without name. And if we call Him the
One, the Good, Spirit, Being itself, Father, God, Creator,
Lord, we do so improperly; instead of pronouncing His name
we are only using the most excellent names we can find
among things that are known, in order to fix our wandering
and disoriented thought.[8] "If it is difficult to know God, it
is impossible to express him." It was Plato who said this in
Timaeus, for he had read the Bible (for Clement there was
no doubt that Pythagoras, Plato and the Stoics had read
the Bible—that they had all borrowed from the sacred book
of the Jews the knowledge they had of God). Being acquainted therefore with the ascent of Moses on Mount Sinai,
Plato knew that, by way of "holy contemplation," Moses
had been able to attain the summit of intelligible things
(ἐπὶ τὴν κορυφὴν τῶν νοητῶν).[9] What is this but that
"region of God" (χώρα τοῦ θεοῦ) which is so difficult
to grasp, what Plato calls the "region of ideas" (χώρα
ἰδεῶν), having learned from Moses that God is a region in
that He contains all things entirely (ὡς τῶν ἁπάντων καὶ
τῶν ὅλων περιεκτικόν).[10] We see Him only from a
distance, as in a mirror and not face to face, by the pure and

---

[5]*Stromateis* V, 11. PG. 9, cols. 101-8.
[6]*Paidagogos* I, 8. PG. 8, col. 336.
[7]*Strom.* II, 2. PG. 8, cols. 936-7.
[8]ibid., V, 12. PG. 9, col. 116.
[9]ibid.
[10]ibid., V, 11. PG. 9, col. 112.

incorporeal flights of thought.[11] In this way Plato and the
sacred scripture, in the thought of Clement of Alexandria,
form an indissoluble amalgam; they are mutually complementary, each one explaining the other.

Having attained to ideas, to the summit of being, we
can by thought grasp that which surpasses these things—i.e.
the Good (ἀγαθόν); in this way, according to Plato, we
attain the very goal of intelligible being.[12] Having reached
this peak Moses entered the darkness (γνόφος), confronted
the invisible and unspeakable. Darkness signifies the disbe-
lief and ignorance of the multitude who cannot know God.
Indeed St. John tells us that "No one has ever seen God.
The Son alone, he who is in the bosom of the of the Father,
has manifested him." The bosom of the Father (κόλπος)
is the invisible and the unspeakable (τὸ ἀόρατον καὶ
ἄρρητον) which Moses met in the darkness. Certain other
thinkers call Him βάθος, depth, abyss, for He contains and
embraces all in His bosom. This explains the passage which
seemed obscure to us, in which Clement made the way of
intellectual analysis end in a flight toward the majesty of
Christ, by which we come to the abyss of the Father "who
contains all" (παντοκράτωρ), being Himself incomprehensible and infinite. The "majesty of Christ" would be then
this "region of ideas," this summit to which Plato accompanies Moses. From there, "through sanctity," we attain the
abyss—the invisible and unspeakable. Is not this "sanctity"
the same as ἀγαθόν, Plato's Good which surpasses the region
of ideas? Moses always finds himself before the unbegotten
(ἀγέννητος) God, the "unknown God" whom St. Paul
preached to the Athenians—the God who cannot be known
except by divine grace and the Word who is with Him.[13]
If Moses asks God to manifest Himself to him it is because
God makes Himself known by power (μόνη τῇ παρ᾽ αὐτοῦ

[11]ibid.
[12]ibid.
[13]ibid., V, 12. PG. 9, col. 116.

δυνάμει γνωστόν). "All intellectual research remains un-sure and blind without the grace of knowledge which comes from God by the Son."[14]

We might expect that Plato would yield here to Moses, that the speculation of the philosopher would be eclipsed by the revelation of God who bestows grace by living in the Son. But it is again Plato who begins to explain to us the nature of grace. We can know God only by the faculties which He bestows. Indeed, says Clement, Plato speaks in *Meno* of a faculty given by God—θεόσδοτον τὴν ἀρετὴν—which is sent to us by divine will (θεία μοίρα). This is nothing other than the "ability to know" (ἕξις γνωστική).[15] We are in the Alexandrian world here, the focal point of eclectic and syncretistic thought, in which revealed religion had long been joined in a grotesque fashion with elements of Hellenistic speculation. One hundred and fifty years be-fore Clement of Alexandria, Philo the Jew had spoken in terms of Platonic philosophy, apropos Moses, of the δυνά-μεις in which God reveals Himself. It is not surprising that in a Christian didactic brought up on Greek philosophy the vision of God is presented as the perfect state of contempla-tion of the eternal being described by Plato.

For Clement Christian perfection consists in the knowl-of the Good and assimilation to God.[16] The Christian goal is to know or see God.[17] In its perfection gnosis is a ἀΐδιος θεωρία, a perpetual contemplation,[18] and in this sense it is superior to faith. If we pass from paganism into faith, then from faith we must rise to gnosis.[19] It is not enough simply to be a Christian in order to have gnosis; this gift must be cultivated by a life devoted to contemplation, by suppressing the passions, by coming to the state of impas-

[14]ibid., col. 109.
[15]ibid., V, 13, cols. 124-5.
[16]ibid., II, 22. PG. 8, col. 1080.
[17]ibid., II, 10. PG. 8, col. 984.
[18]ibid., IV, 22. PG. 8, col. 1345.
[19]ibid., VII, 10. PG. 9, cols. 480-1.

sibility—ἀπάθεια. The ascetic ideal of ἀπάθεια, in
Clement's words, does not differ significantly from the impassibility of the Stoics. Only a perfect Christian who has
attained ἀπάθεια possesses the gift of knowledge, is a
true gnostic. Here it should be noted that Clement's "gnostic"
has nothing to do with the so-called gnostic heretics, whom
Clement fought as "false gnostics." Furthermore, in Clement's
thought, Christian gnostics definitely do not form a race
apart, to be distinguished by their spiritual nature from the
rest of men who are necessarily carnal or psychic. They are
Christians who have, by exercising the faculty of contemplation, acquired the perfection intended for all. "The gnostic,"
says Clement, "in so far as he loves the one true God, is a
perfect man, a friend of God, established in the status of
son. These titles of rank, knowledge and perfection spring
from the vision of God (κατὰ τὴν τοῦ θεοῦ ἐποπτείαν),
the supreme benefit received by a gnostic soul who has become perfectly pure, having been made worthy of beholding
eternally and face to face, as the Scripture says, God who
contains all."[20] This is the vision of God the Father, of the
invisible God, the abyss which contains in its bosom the
majesty of the Word and the world of ideas. It is the vision
reserved for the "pure in heart," for gnostics who have come
to the final perfection. But few men can attain the fullness
of gnosis.[21] The majority live on milk, on imperfect knowledge, the knowledge of the catechism, the faith of those
who are simple-minded or carnal. But the clear revelation
of the age to come, the vision "face to face," is solid food.[22]
It is impossible in this world and only gnosis can achieve
it after death.

Clement's portrait of the gnostic, however, gives the impression that even in this life he enjoys that perfect knowledge which leaves no room for mystery.[23] As examples of

[20]ibid., VII, 11. PG. 9, col. 496.
[21]ibid., V, 1. PG. 9, col. 17.
[22]*Paidagogos* I, 6. PG. 8, col. 293.
[23]*Strom.* VI, 8. PG. 9, cols. 289-92.

true gnostics Clement lists James, Peter, John, Paul and the other apostles. The gnostic knows all, understands all (πάντων περιλεπτικόν), even what seems incomprehensible to others.[24] Is it not true that gnosis is a faculty of the reasoning soul, exercised in order to establish man—by way of knowledge—in immortality?[25]

The contemplation of God is presented therefore as the highest bliss, and this contemplation seems to involve man's intellectual faculty almost exclusively. Knowledge is beatitude. It would seem that we are very far here from Irenaeus' eschatological vision of God, and that a rift has been made within the idea of beatitude itself: on the one hand the incorruptible life of the blessed, who participate in the eternal light of the Father shed by the glorified Christ; on the other hand this gnosis, an intellectual theory, a comprehension of the incomprehensible, which Clement extols as the ultimate goal of perfected Christians. Indeed we cannot help noticing the split between the living God of the Bible and the God of Platonic contemplation, a split which disrupts the very integrity of eternal bliss, when we hear Clement declaring: "I will say boldly that he who pursues gnosis for the sake of divine knowledge itself will not embrace it simply because he wishes to be saved. Intellect, in its proper use, tends always to be an activity; and this ever-active intellect, having become in its uninterrupted tension the essential feature of the gnostic, is transformed into eternal contemplation and exists as a living substance. If therefore we should suggest hypothetically that the gnostic choose between knowledge of God and eternal salvation, assuming that these two things are separate (in fact they are absolutely identical), he will without hesitation choose the knowledge of God."[26]

Whatever Clement may say, the contemplation of God (γνῶσις τοῦ θεοῦ) and eternal salvation (σωτηρία ἡ

---

[24]ibid.
[25]ibid.
[26]ibid., IV, 22. PG. 8, cols. 1345-8.

αἰώνιος) are actually separated here, if only in thought,
and gnosis is exalted above salvation. In vain does he say
that faith is raised to gnosis by love (ἀγάπη), for this
ἀγάπη is eclipsed by γνῶσις, and it is precisely gnosis
which occupies that place in the age to come which St. Paul
reserves exclusively for ἀγάπη. Clement's notion of gnosis
reminds us of certain passages in *Poimandres,* the collection
of so-called hermetic tracts written in Egypt, in which knowledge is presented as a deifying formula by which one is
raised to the sphere of the fixed stars.[27] Thought, not separated
from the divine essence, leads men to God;[28] in this way man
attains salvation by a knowledge superior to faith. Clement
mentions the writings of Hermes Trismegistus,[29] but he never
quotes them, so far as I know. If he does not explicitly formulate the doctrine of the vision of the essence of God, it is
because this term (οὐσία) has not yet been used to designate the one nature of three persons. But all the doctrinal
elements are present in the thought of Clement of Alexandria
to support the affirmation that gnostics contemplate the
essence of God (for Clement the divine essence would be the
equivalent of the abyss of the παντοκράτωρ).

Thus the theme of the contemplation of God which must
inevitably be raised in Christian thought is presented first in
a form not free from accretions alien to Christianity. Clement's
gnostics, who form the inner—one might even say esoteric—
circle of the Church, are in his thought perfect Christians,
the saints who live in constant communion with God. Their
life must almost inevitably end in martyrdom. We recognize
here the ideal of sanctity held by Christians in the age of
persecution. But the portrait of the gnostic man is not drawn
to life: it does not reproduce the concrete figure of the
saint. It is a literary fiction; Clement is providing a Christian
disguise for the intellectualistic contemplative whom he had

[27]*Corpus Hermeticum,* Budé's collection, Vol. 1, Treatise X, p. 112f.
[28]ibid., Treatise XII, p. 173f.
[29]*Strom.* IV, 4. PG. 9, col. 253.

found outside the experience of the Church's life. Concrete data from the ascetic life will be necessary to replace this Platonic utopia by a truly Christian practice of contemplation, which will return, under a new aspect, to the eschatological vision of St. Irenaeus.

* * *

The thought of Origen (*c.* 185-254 or 255) is more precise, less fluid than that of Clement, under whom Origen studied for a while at the Alexandrian Didascalion. Clement was more a moralist; Origen is a theologian and at the same time an exegete, apologist and master of the ascetical life. For him also Christians are divided into two categories: those who believe and those who know. But every Christian must strive to know. Also the revelation is addressed both to the simple-minded and to the perfect. To the former it offers moral instruction, to the rest "gnosis," instruction concerning the Trinity or "theology."[30] God is revealed through the sacred words of Scripture to the extent that we detach ourselves from the literal sense—all that is within reach of the Jews—in order to penetrate the spiritual sense accessible to Christians. But here too there are gradations. When St. Paul speaks to the Corinthians as an unlearned person, wishing to preach nothing other than Christ crucified, he is speaking to the simple-minded. In contrast, St. John, when he speaks in the prologue of his Gospel of the divine Logos, is addressing those who are capable of knowing.[31] In general whatever is connected with the humanity of Christ belongs to *economy*; it is intended for the faith of the simple-minded. Whatever is connected with the divinity of Christ is in the domain of theology reserved for the perfect, those skilled in contemplation.

These two different stages of perfection are realized in

[30]*In Lev.* XIII, 3. PG. 12, col. 547.
[31]*In Io.* I, 7, 43. PG. 14, cols. 36-7.

two types of life: the active life and the contemplative life
(this distinction is borrowed from the Stoics). Origen was
the first to make Martha and Mary, in the Gospel of St.
Luke, figures of the active and contemplative life.[32] The
"active people" stand in the outer courtyard of the Temple;
contemplatives enter into the house of God.[33] The different
parts of the temple of Jerusalem correspond to the degrees
of perfection in knowledge. Thus the doors which separate
the sanctuary from the outer courtyard are the doors of
knowledge. There is the first contemplation, the contemplation of corporeal or incorporeal beings. The Holy of Holies
is then the knowledge of God.[34] Christians must therefore
climb to three levels: first πρακτική—the struggle for ἀπάθεια and love; second the φυσικὴ θεωρία—the knowledge
of the mysteries of creation; and third θεολογία—the knowledge of God in the Λόγος. Exegete above all, Origen returns to the Scriptures to assign to those in the first stage
the book of Proverbs, the book of moral precepts; and to
those in second stage, Ecclesiastes, which discovers the vanity
of created being and urges us to seek the knowledge of
God; and finally to those of the third stage, the Song of
Songs, which, in celebrating the nuptials of the human soul
with the Logos, instructs us in the contemplation of God.

It is then the third degree of *theology* which particularly
interests us in Origen's extremely rich and complex thought.
What is this *theology,* this knowledge of God in the Word,
which is for Origen the contemplation of God and at the
same time the supreme degree of Christian perfection?

Perfection consists in being assimilated to God. The
philosophers have spoken rightly of this truth, but they
did not find it themselves: they borrowed it from the holy
books of the Jews, where Moses teaches us in Genesis that
man is created in the image and likeness of God. The image

[32]*Fragments from the Commentary on St. John,* No. 80, CGS. 10, 547.
[33]*In Ps. CXXXIII.* PG. 12, col. 1652.
[34]*In Ps. CXVII.* PG. 12, col. 1581.

appears to us now; the likeness is a possibility of perfection which will reach its term in the consummation of time, when God will be all in all.[35] Origen defines this ultimate state of perfection a little later on: "That God will be all in all signifies that he will be all, and in each one. And in each one he will be all in the sense that the whole reasoning mind, purified of all the filth of vice, washed of all stain of malice, will feel, understand and think as God; in the sense that he will no longer see anything but God, that he will possess God, that God will be the mode and measure of all his movements—it is thus that God will be all."[36] It is the deified state or union with God, realized by the exclusion of every other aim of perfection. God becomes all, in such a way that the human mind no longer knows anything other than Him. If the human mind is made "one mind with God," according to the word of St. Paul (who appears frequently in Origen's writing), it is because in the totality of consciousness the mind comprehends God, who becomes its sole content. Deification is realized by contemplation. God becomes all in all by the knowledge of each.

Naturally this knowledge is inseparable from love. Origen was too good an exegete to forget the place of ἀγάπη in the vision of God in St. John and St. Paul. As knowledge increases love becomes more and more fervent.[37] This is why the word ψυχή, soul, which Origen derived from ψῦχος, cold, denoted for him a chilled spiritual substance which has lost its primitive fervor and become estranged from God.

The primitive state in which man was created corresponds to his final state, i.e. to God who has by contemplation become all in all. Indeed when Genesis speaks of the creation of heaven "in the beginning" and when it teaches us then that the firmament was created the day following, it is referring to these two different heavens: the spiritual and the

[35] *De principiis* III, 6, i. PG. 11, col. 333
[36] ibid., III, 6, 3. PG. 11, col. 356.
[37] ibid., I, 3, 8. PG. 11, col. 155.

corporeal. "The first heaven," says Origen, "which we have
qualified as spiritual, is our mind[38] (νοῦς or *mens*) which
is essentially spiritual, in other words, it is our spiritual home,
which beholds and contemplates God; and the corporeal
heaven is that which beholds with the eyes of the body."[39]
"The external man" is already a degradation from the perfect state, the state of the spiritual man. The second day of
creation, with the idea of number and multiplicity, is a loss
of unity, a descent to an inferior level. It marks the beginning
of time. From this point on creation is accompanied, in
Origen's thought, by a fall of the perfect beings created "in
the the beginning," a fall into a temporal and material existence. The "beginning" (ἀρχή), in which God created in
the first day, is the Word (Λόγος). Also the creation of the
first day is a non-temporal act before time, or rather outside of time. It is inexact to speak of the pre-existence of
souls in Origen's doctrine, for the idea of a temporal suc-
cession, with a "before" and "after," cannot apply to the
relationship between eternity and time. It is a question rather
of an eternal creation within the Logos, of a purely spiritual
primitive existence and its degradation or physical deformation as a result of a fall. The vision of God was the true
existence of spiritual beings created in the Logos; God was
the content of this perfect spiritual life.[40] In abandoning it
the spiritual beings ceased to be what they were. The mind
(νοῦς or *mens*) moves from the spiritual plane, it becomes
soul, ψυχή, i.e. a being within the historical process, so
that by contemplation it might recover its primitive state,
the state of pure spirit.[41]

While it is a degraded spiritual substance, the soul re-
tains nevertheless a certain relationship or co-nature (συγ-

[38]The French word *esprit* includes the meanings of the words "mind,"
"spirit," and "intellect" in English. Where any of these words appear in
the text that follows the reader is invited to keep this cluster of meanings
in mind. [Translator.]
[39]*1st Hom. on Genesis* 2. *Sources chrétiennes* 7, p. 65.
[40]*De principiis* II, 6, 3. PG. 11, col. 211.
[41]ibid., II, 8, 3. PG. 11, cols. 222-3.

γένεια) with the divine Word, in so far as it keeps its reasonable being, the λογικὸν εἶναι which makes it participate in the Logos and renders it in His image.[42] The perfection of the image (εἰκὼν) is the likeness (ὁμοίωσις) which is the vision of God—the primitive as well as the final state of the spirit. The return to the vision of God in the Logos (θεολογία) restores the likeness and realizes the perfect union with God, who again becomes "all in all."

For Origen this union with God seems to be so intimate and indissoluble that he affirms the reality of the hypostatic union between divinity and humanity in Christ and tries to explain it by the vision of God possessed by the soul of the Incarnate Christ. It must not be forgotten that for Origen this soul of Christ, or rather His spirit, existed before, i.e. exists outside the Incarnation. It had never fallen like human souls, like other spirits, and it remains eternally united to the Word in the act of the vision of God. Therefore the Incarnation of Christ represents the unique union of this perfect soul or spirit with a human body, a union by virtue of which the eternal Word enters voluntarily into the historic process and becomes man.[43] Since Christ's soul does not cease to behold God in the Logos, His body exists in the Logos, deified and spiritualized. Origen was the first to formulate the doctrine which will later be called "perichoretic," or, the doctrine of the "communication of idioms." This co-penetration of corporal, spiritual and divine qualities is realized, for him, in the person of Christ Incarnate, by the vision of God. It is the vision of God which deifies Christ's humanity and also deifies our humanity for us in His.

In becoming man Christ entered into full union with human nature.[44] In building the Church He reunited her in Himself as the dispersed members of a body.[45] "As long as we are in sin and not yet perfect, He is in us only in

[42]*De principiis* IV, 36. PG. 11, cols. 411-12.
[43]ibid., II, 6, 3. PG. 11, col. 211.
[44]*In Io.* 10, 41.
[45]*Homily VII on Leviticus* 2.

part and this is why we know in part, and prophesy in part,
until each member attains the measure spoken of by the
Apostle: 'I live, yet no longer I, but Christ lives in me.' "
This progressive union with Christ, accomplished in the body
of the Church, represents for Origen the mystical nuptials
of the human soul with the divine Logos, described allegor-
ically in the Song of Songs. In this union man acquires, beside
his mortal, corruptible and human senses, another sense
(αἴσθησις) which is immortal, spiritual and divine:[46] "a
new sight with which to contemplate supra-corporeal objects;
a hearing capable of distinguishing the voices which do not
resound in the air, a taste to savor the living bread coming
down from heaven, a sense of smell which perceives the realities which led Paul to say 'the fragrant odor of Christ,'
the sense of touch which John possessed when he said that
he had handled with his hands the Word of life."[47] We can
see here the first outline of a doctrine of the spiritual senses.[48]
This doctrine will find its later development, for example,
in the works of Gregory of Nyssa. As for Origen, his
radical spiritualism keeps him from making wider use of
this idea of the spiritualized or transfigured senses in relation to the perception of divine realities. In the Περὶ ἀρχῶν
he returns again to this point and notes that we often attribute faculties to the soul which belong to the organs of
sense; thus in saying that we see with the eyes of the heart
we are expressing the fact that the intellectual faculty con-
ceives something intelligible.[49] If it is said that "No one
has ever seen God," this signifies, for beings endowed with
intellect, that He is invisible to the eyes. For it is one thing
to see, another to know. To be seen and to see belong to
corporeal realities; to be known and to know belong to in-

[46]De principiis I, 1, 8. PG. 11, col. 129c.

[47]Contra Celsum PG. 11, col. 749AB.

[48]cf. Rahner, "The Origin of a Doctrine of Five Spiritual Senses in the
Writings of Origen." RAM, 1932, pp. 113-45.

[49]De principiis, I, 1, 9. PG. 11, cols. 129-30.

telligible natures.[50] All that we can sense or conceive of God will only be one tiny spark of light, it can give us no idea at all of the excellence of the divine nature.[51] Here the idea of the spark appears for the first time in Christian literature. This is a theme which will be developed in the West and will occupy a central place in the system of Meister Eckhart, although in a completely different context, having nothing in common with the doctrine of the spiritual senses.

In his twenty-seventh homily on Numbers, Origen interprets the "stations" of the people of Israel in the desert as stages on the road toward the vision of God. It is the exodus of the soul, which is delivered progressively from corporeal attachments. At first the temptations are merged with the first experiences of the divine. The Word comforts the soul by visions or visitations which undoubtedly correspond to the perception of the divine by the spiritual senses—the first contacts of the soul with God. But at more elevated levels the visions cease, making room for gnosis, for illumination of the purely intellectual order which tends to become and is even already a contemplation—θεωρία. However the intellectual elements in gnosis appear only at first; they are obliterated more and more, to the extent that the soul is united with Christ and the spiritual marriage (πνευματικὸς γάμος) with the Logos is accomplished. This marriage is not the pinnacle of the soul's ascent. It has been freed from the corporeal domain, it has gone beyond the intelligible, the celestial spheres;[52] but if it has been assimilated to Christ, if it has become "of one mind" with the Logos, it is to see in Him the invisible God. In the Logos the soul is an image (εἰκών); by the vision of God it recovers the likeness (ὁμοίωσις), becomes fully spirit again, is deified. Indeed "if the spirit once purified has transcended all that is material, it is in order to bring the contemplation

[50]ibid., 8, cols. 128-9.
[51]*De principiis* I, 1, 5. PG. 11, col. 124.
[52]*Contra Celsum* VI, 20. PG. 11, cols. 1320-1.

of God to its proper fulfilment and to be deified by that which it contemplates" (ἐπεὶ ὁ κεκαθαρμένος καὶ ὑπεραναβὰς πάντα ὑλικὰ νοῦς, ἵνα ἀκριβώσῃ τὴν θεωρίαν τοῦ θεοῦ, ἐν οἷς θεωρεῖ, θεοποιεῖται).[53] Thus the restoration of the first state, in which the soul—ψυχὴ—becomes once more spirit—νοῦς—is effected by the union with the only Son in the vision of God.[54] "There will be then," says Origen, "only one activity in those who come to God by the Word who is with God, i.e. the activity of knowing him, in order to form in this way, in knowledge of the Father, precisely one Son, since the Son is the only one who has known the Father."[55]

Some critics (Volker) have maintained that in this union (in one only Son contemplating the Father) human spirits are completely identified with Christ in Origen's thought, are in fact depersonalized. This would seem to be a spontaneous ecstatic state and the suppression of personal consciousness. Mr. Puech, in his criticism of Volker's work, and Lieske in a work on the mysticism of the Logos in Origen,[56] demonstrate with evidence that Origen was far from professing such a concept of union with the Logos. The word "ecstacy" in his writing almost always has a pejorative meaning, that of alienation, of loss of mental equilibrium. Speaking of the psychic states which suggest ecstacy in the positive sense of this word, he uses the expression "sober intoxication" (νηφάλιος μέθη), an oxymoron borrowed from Philo, and one which will be made much of in Christian literature. The divine Logos by no means supplants man's consciousness, but transports the spirit outside human realities. For Origen, man can cease to be man in the course of this evolution ending in spiritual existence, but he certainly does not lose his personal self-consciousness in this process.

[53]In Io. XXXII, 17. PG. 14, col. 817A.
[54]De principiis III, 6, 3. PG. 11, cols. 335-6; In Io. I, 16. PG. 14, cols. 49-52.
[55]In Io. I, 16. PG. 14, cols. 49-52.
[56]Theologie der Logosmystik bei Origenes, Münster, 1938.

The Word is the final stage, and yet a stage which must lead to the vision of God. If the Word is "with God," this means that He is God; and He would not be truly God if He was not with God and did not behold without ceasing the abyss of the Father.[57] Likewise those who have been created in the image of the Logos become gods by enjoying this vision with Him. It is not at all *by* the Logos, by His mediation, but in Him and with Him, that the spirits who have attained perfection see the Father in a vision or direct knowledge.

It must be noted here that, for Origen, while the Son is of one essence with the Father and is God by essence (κατ' οὐσίαν) and not by participation, He is not in the least inferior to the Father, a God of the second order, or subordinated to the Father as the instrument of His manifestation. "It is said: Whoever has seen the Father, has seen me." Therefore, we can see Him in no way other than by beginning with the Son, by ascending from the Son to the Father. As the steps in the temple lead to the holy of holies, the Son contains in Himself these steps from His humanity toward His divinity, toward "He who is." There is a certain gradation in the knowledge of God; we do not attain perfect knowledge of the Father by inverting this order. Thus we cannot see the Father in order subsequently to know Wisdom or Truth; but beginning with Wisdom and Truth we ascend to the Father of Wisdom. Having first known the Truth we then come to see the essence or the power and nature of God superior to this essence.[58]

Like Clement, Origen teaches us what is the object of the contemplation of God, the ultimate goal of the θεωρία, of the θεολογία. It is the very essence or the "property and nature of God which surpasses essence," which perfected spirits, reconstituted in their primitive state, behold (or rather know) with the only Son, being united to the Son in

[57]*In Io.* II, 2, col. 109.
[58]ibid., 19, I, col. 536c.

categorical terms, even more outspoken than those of Clement
and Origen, to express the unknowable nature of the οὐσία:
"invisible, incomprehensible even in the eyes of the seraphim
(ἀόρατος καὶ σεραφικοῖς ὀφθαλμοῖς ἀπερίληπτος),
not to be contained either in a thought or a place (λόγῳ
καὶ τόπῳ ἀχώρητος), in no way divided in its powers
(δυνάμει ἀμερής), intangible (ἀναφής), without dimensions, without depth (ἀμεγέθης, ἀβαθὴς—against Clement
and Origen, for whom the Logos is μέγεθος and the Father
βάθος), without amplitude (ἄπλατης), without form
(ἀνείδεος) ... far surpassing in brilliance the whole light
of the heavens, how much more sublime than all that is on
high, infinitely surpassing also all spirit by its spiritual
nature."[1]

What remains of Origen in the thought of Didymus is
the tendency to intellectualize the spiritual senses. If God is
light, it is not the eye but thought (νόησις) which perceives
its brilliance.[2] All scriptural anthropomorphisms must be dis-
carded in speaking of God. Thus the Face is the Divinity
(θειότης) existing before the world. God's back is creation, and the acts of providence in which God is manifested.
However, while the vision of God receives an intellectualistic
emphasis in Didymus, knowledge being acquired through
thought, nevertheless the essence or nature of God will no
longer (as in Origen's thought) be an eminently simple intelligible substance, but super-essential essence or nature
(ὑπερούσιος οὐσία, ὑπερούσιος φύσις)[3] and, in this
sense, the nature of the Trinity remains inaccessible to all
created knowledge, even to angels and archangels.[4] In this
way, in the thought of a fourth century anti-Arian theologian
of the Origenistic school who confessed the consubstantial
God of the Trinity, Origen's intellectualism is at least limited,
if not completely overcome.

[1]*De Trinitate*, I, 16. PG. 39, col. 332c.
[2]*In Io*. PG. 39, col. 1645c.
[3]*De Trinitatis*, 4, 4, col. 484A.
[4]ibid., I, 36, col. 440A; II, 4, col. 481A.

this act of vision. While He is of the essence of the Father, as Origen says, the Son may seem to be only a kind of stepping stone toward the vision of the essence. This is because, for Origen, the Father represents the essence itself, the primary simplicity of the divine nature. It is this divine nature, the Father, or, simply, God, who is the object of deifying contemplation in the age to come. And Origen tells us elsewhere[59] that God's is "a simple nature, suffering within itself no adjunction": "In all ways a Monad and, therefore, Unity and Spirit, he is the source from which all intellectual or spiritual nature takes its beginning." "The simplicity of the divine nature... consists therefore in one single form (species) only, the form of divinity."

So we see (on the basis of our study of Origen's writing) that the vision of God in His essence is presented within the framework of an intellectualistic doctrine in which vision means knowledge (gnosis) and knowledge is equated, in the last analysis, with the contemplation of intelligible realities. We are a long way here from the eschatological vision of St. Irenaeus, where the eternal light of the Father appears in the glorious body of the Son in order to confer on resurrected men the incorruptibility of eternal life and participation in the divine life. A new theme of mystical contemplation appears in Alexandrian theology, but it still depends too much on the intellectualistic ideal of Platonic contemplation.

It is unjust to speak of the "Platonism of the Fathers" every time the subject of contemplation is raised and there is a desire, as we see in Nygren, to limit the truly Christian vision of God to the eschatological manifestation alone. The problem of communion with God in contemplation ought to be raised in Christian experience. Contemplation is not the exclusive appanage of Platonism and if it were, Platonism in a broad sense would simply mean spirituality which tends toward communion with eternal realities, where the degrees

[59]*De principiis,* I, 1, 6. PG. 11, cols. 124-6.

of contemplation correspond to the progressive deification of human beings immersed in the contingent. In this very broad sense almost all religious speculation would be an unconscious Platonism. In any case all religious thought of the Mediterranean world of the first centuries of our era has been Platonic in this sense.

Christianity could not fail to respond to this universal aspiration, demonstrating the path of Christian contemplation in which communion with the living God, the personal God of revelation, is realized. The first attempt to make such a response was carried out by apologists like Clement and Origen, too anxious to show pagans that all the treasures of Hellenistic wisdom were contained and surpassed in the "true philosophy" of the Church. Involuntarily they brought about a kind of synthesis, lending to Christian contemplation an accent of Platonic intellectualism and spiritualism alien to the spirit of the Gospel.

In Origen's writing the vision of the essence of God, the knowledge of God in His essence, involves a substratum of intellectualistic thought: a contemplation of God as an intelligible nature, eminently simple; a conception of man as a spiritual being *par excellence,* related to the God-essence as the source of intelligible beings—his physical and corporal nature being an anomaly, something which must finally disappear, be reabsorbed into the spiritual substance, into the νοῦς living by the contemplation of God. The whole richness of created being is the result of a deformation, a degradation of spiritual natures. The notion of created being itself is not clear. It seems that the line of demarcation, for Origen, passes between the spiritual domain related to God and the psychomaterial world, rather than between the Being who is divine by nature and beings created out of nothing. His God is a God of spirits especially, and not the God of all flesh. He is a God of beings endowed with intellect, indeed a God of intellectual beings in the strict sense of this term. When Origen speaks to us of the intel-

lectual work of those who search into the reasons of things,
a work which will continue for the saints after death, in
the terrestrial paradise which he calls "the place of erudition"
(*locus eruditionis*), "the auditorium or school of souls"
(*auditorium vel scola animarum*), he makes us smile at
his professor's school-room paradise. Having received our
instruction in this school, we are to carry on higher studies
in different *mansiones,* which the Greeks call spheres and
the Scripture calls heavens. Here in a state of purity we will
examine "face to face" the causes of created beings, before
seeing God, i.e. "knowing him through the intellect and in
purity of heart" (*videre Deum, id est intelligere per puritatem
cordis*).[60] Having become acquainted with the intelligible
causes of created beings, the "pure in heart" who are search-
ing into the nature of God are more like learned scholars
than saints of the Church.

But we must not be unjust. Origen's personality is too
rich to be expressed solely in an intellectualistic doctrine of
the vision of God. Alongside the intellectualistic Origen of
the Περὶ ἀρχῶν and the apology *Against Celsus* there is
another Origen, the Origen of the commentaries on the Song
of Songs and the Gospel of St. John and the homilies. An
Origen fervent and touching, not at all doctrinaire, bent over
the well of vision which the study of Holy Scripture has
suddenly opened up in his soul; one would be tempted to
say a mystical Origen, if this word had not been almost
emptied of meaning by being made to mean too much. He
was a speculative Greek accustomed to intellectual contemplation and at the same time an ardent Christian, preaching
martyrdom for Christ, seeking a concrete realization of communion with God in a life of asceticism and prayer. The
Greek intellectual sometimes disappears in the face of the
disciple of Jesus, for example when Origen tells us that
action and contemplation, practice and gnosis are united in

[60]ibid., 2, 11, cols. 240-8.

a single act—in prayer. This is already a departure, an exit from the world of Platonic contemplation.

However this may be, we must recognize together with Fr. Festugière that the Hellenistic world enters the Church with Clement and Origen, bringing with it elements alien to the Christian tradition—elements of religious speculation and intellectualistic spirituality belonging to a world altogether different from that of the Gospel. A world altogether different, and yet also the same, for the pagans and Christians of Alexandria. Can we ever define just how much a Christian belongs to the Church and to what extent he participates by his thought, feelings and reactions in the life of the world in which he is immersed? We must not imagine that Christians and pagans lived in water-tight compartments, especially in Alexandria where both participated in the same culture, in the same intellectual life. Origen and Plotinus had together attended the lectures of Ammonius Saccas, the founder of the neo-Platonic school. The two men knew and respected one another. Porphyry reports, in his life of Plotinus, that Origen came one day to his lecture. "Plotinus flushed and was about to get up; begged by Origen to speak, he said that people no longer feel like speaking when they are sure that they will be addressing those who know what it is they are going to say; he continued the discussion for a little while and then got up to leave."[61] Both men, the pagan philosopher and the Christian theologian, develop on parallel courses and in different religious frameworks the same themes of Hellenistic spirituality, of the escape or flight out of the world of senses. This celestial journey is accomplished not on foot, says Plotinus, but by contemplation which assimilates the soul to God, which restores in it the likeness by leading it back to its native land, where the Father awaits it. Porphyry says that Plotinus, "by the grace of the illumination which teaches by way of intelligence . . . saw God, who has neither

[61] *Life of Plotinus,* published as an introduction to the Enneads. Budé's Collection, I, pp. 15-16.

form nor essence for he exists beyond intelligence and the intelligible. . . . The goal and end was for him intimate union with the God who is above all things. While I was with him he attained this goal four times, thanks to an inexpressible working and not by his own efficacy."[62] There is the same intellectual world, an almost identical spirituality, in both Plotinus and Origen, in both the pagan and Christian contemplatives of Alexandria. It is not a matter of borrowings or influences; the two spiritualities were formed simultaneously. It is a question rather of a natural kinship, of the same cultural tradition, expressed not only in the community of language and a common methodology, but also in the same deep-rooted attitude toward the ultimate goal of man. Instead of Christianizing Hellenistic spirituality, Clement and Origen almost succeeded in spiritualizing Christianity. But thanks to them this Hellenistic spirituality, this intellectualistic or super-intellectualistic mysticism, once introduced into the circle of the Church, will later be consumed, transformed from top to bottom, surpassed. Centuries of struggle and superhuman effort will be required to go beyond Hellenism, by liberating it from its natural attachments and its ethnic and cultural limitations, before it will finally become a universal form of Christian truth, the very language of the Church. If this struggle is connected especially with the name of Origen, it must also be said that it began within the restless and complex soul of this great Alexandrian master. Those who have attacked his doctrine as well as those who have followed it have all sought to transform his intellectualism—on the dogmatic plane especially, where Platonic conceptions are crystalized by Origen into the spiritualistic doctrine of preexistent souls who have fallen into psycho-material existence and who return to their original state by way of contemplation. In its reaction against Origenism Christian theology will keep the vocabulary proper to the thought of Alexandria, but it will separate itself more

[62]ibid., pp. 26-7.

and more from the point of departure of this thought, as it was shared by both Plotinus and Origen. Salvation by means of a flight out of the world, an escape of the spirit from the world, will appear as a limitation or spiritualistic deformation. In reality we are dealing with a way of salvation which does not tear us out of the world but is rather opened *for* this created world, in the Word become flesh. Gnosis, intellectual or super-intellectual contemplation will be seen, more and more, as but one of the necessary moments of the communion of created beings with God, without being the way of deifying union par excellence.

* * *

In Alexandria itself, St. Athanasius (293-373) will speak less of the vision of God than of the deification (θέωσις) to which created beings are called. In one of his early works, the Sermon against the Gentiles,[63] in which certain reminders of Origen can still be recognized, St. Athanasius speaks of Adam as of an ecstastic who "being raised in all his purity above sensible things and every obstacle to divine gnosis, contemplates ceaselessly the image of the Father, the God-Word, in whose image he is made." However, the vision of God which Adam received in the earthly paradise is given an altogether different emphasis in the thought of Athanasius than in the writings of Origen. In his treatise *On the Incarnation*[64] this vision appears as a necessary condition for the total deification of Adam. If he had been able to retain the divine likeness by contemplating God, he would have destroyed all possibility of corruption in his created nature and would have become forever incorruptible. As in St. Irenaeus, vision signifies here a certain participation in the incorruptible state, a stability of the being participating in the creative nature of the Logos. "Neither the sun," he says

[63]*Cont. Gent.*, 2. PG. 25, cols. 5C-8B.
[64]*De Inc.*, 4. PG. 25, col. 104C.

further on, "nor the moon, nor the heavens, nor water, nor
the ether have strayed out of their appointed way; but,
thanks to the knowledge of the Logos, their creator and king
(ἀλλ᾿ εἰδότες τὸν ἑαυτοῦ δημιουργὸν καὶ βασιλέα
Λόγον), they remain as they were created."[65] Athanasius
distinguishes two moments in the act of creation itself: the
production of created being, and God's entry into the world
or the presence of the Logos in creatures which confers on
each created being a mark, a sign of divine adoption. This
is the principle by which God makes Himself known in His
works, at the same time that a faculty for participating in
the Logos is introduced into created being. By the Incarnation the Logos will become the principle of a new life. He
will become again "the beginning of the divine ways in his
works." There is here a new creation—in which the resurrected body of Christ becomes the origin of the incorruptibility of created beings. "The Word was made a *bearer
of the flesh* (σαρκοφόρος), in order that men might become *bearers of the Spirit* (πνευματοφόροι)."[66] If the
Holy Spirit confers on us "the celestial life," by making us
capable of knowledge, of the "gnosis of the Father and the
Son,"[67] this knowledge will no longer be the source but the
fruit of our assimilation to the Word. It will not be the
intellectualistic gnosis of Clement's gnostics or of Origen's
spiritual men by which we will obtain incorruptibility. The
Christian ideal, for St. Athanasius, is no longer a Hellenistic
utopia, it has nothing in common with the flight of the
Platonists. St. Athanasius finds it in the life of the Church,
within Egypt itself. The *Life of St. Anthony* which he wrote
(and there is no serious reason to doubt its authenticity)
gives us a concrete example of an anchorite of Thebaid
achieving communion with God in the struggle for incorruptibility. The contemplation of God in the Platonic sense

[65]ibid., 43, col. 172BC.
[66]*De Inc. et cont. Arian.*, 8. PG. 26, col. 991C.
[67]*Letter to the Bishops of Egypt and Libya,* I. PG. 25, col. 540A.

of the word—and even the vision of God as the goal of the solitary life—seems completely alien to this spirituality of the desert. It is a spiritual environment altogether different from the intellectual world of Alexandria, the world of Origen and Plotinus. It is precisely this environment which represents for St. Athanasius the realization of the Christian ideal: i.e. communion with God in the Incarnate Word, in Christ who has conquered sin and death by communicating to created nature the premises of incorruptibility and future deification.

CHAPTER FOUR

The Cappadocians

On the dogmatic plane the reaction against Origenism enters a new phase in the fourth century in the Arian controversies. It is not easy to define this reaction against the spirit of Origenism, a reaction that can be felt through all the vicissitudes of the anti-Arian struggle. This is all the more true in that among the defenders of consubstantiality there were theologians, like St. Alexander of Alexandria or Didymus the Blind, who were more or less closely connected with Origen's thought. It would be unjust to regard Origen's subordinationism as the source of the Arian heresy, and yet the radical reaction to the problem raised by Arianism was bound to eliminate forever the subordination of Origen's school. If the Logos is consubstantial with the Father it is no longer possible to speak of the Father as a simple substance, as God in Himself. When the essence or nature of God is mentioned, it can no longer refer to the abyss (βάθος) of the Father approached through the Son, and contemplated with the Son through unity with Him. When God is spoken of now it will be the one essence in three hypostases, the indivisible Trinity, which will be presented to the mind.

Even for Didymus the Blind (313-93), who makes use of Origen, the unknowable nature of God is no longer applied to the person of the Father but to the divine essence as such, to the οὐσία of the Trinity. And he will use very

Origen's intellectualism will find itself in friendly territory among the Arians, where subordinationism degenerates into a radical dissimilarity between the Father and the Son, identifies the divine nature with the Father and ejects the Son into the realm of created being. The extreme faction in Arianism, the "Anomoeans," professed a clearly defined intellectualism in the question of the knowledge of God. This is why the disputes against Eunomius (365 and 385) have had a great importance for Christian gnosiology in general and consequently also for the doctrines of the vision of God.

For Eunomius the Father was a perfect monad, "God who is infinitely unique," admitting no participation whatsoever in His divinity, no progress out of His unique οὐσία toward the three hypostases. Generation means a corruption of the simple essence, and can signify therefore nothing but creation. The absolute simplicity of the οὐσία is opposed to any distinction, even a virtual distinction, in the divine attributes. It would seem that such a notion of simplicity would be bound to lead to agnosticism. Indeed Arius, who started with this same idea, denied the possibility of knowing the Father, denied this possibility even to the Son. But Eunomius professed a gnosiological optimism which led him to say, according to the historian Socrates, that he knew the essence of God as well as he himself was known, and in dealing with his adversaries he quoted the text of St. John (4: 22): "You worship what you do not know, we worship what we know."

For Eunomius there are two types of names which designate objects of knowledge. First, invented names, conceived by human thought, by reflection (κατ' ἐπίνοιαν), imagined names, conventional signs having no objective value, giving no knowledge of the object itself. If a man is reduced to this class of names, he remains mute, incapable of expressing any reality. But there are other names which are not at all the product of human reflection. These are objective names, so to speak, expressing the very essence of objects; they are

rational name-revelations. The concept revealing the intelligible content, i.e. the essence of things, is found by analyzing
these names. Since the true name is that which expresses the
essence of a being, only God gives such names to things.
There is here a philosophy of language, and at the same
time a theory of knowledge based on Platonism combined
with the Stoic doctrine of "seminal words." The words of
command with which the God of Genesis created the world
are the seeds which logically produce the things created,
and at the same time names sown in the human soul. A
similar doctrine is formulated by Cratylus in Plato's dialogue
by the same name.

As applied to the knowledge of God, the gnosiology of
Eunomius reveals an intellectualism pushed to the extreme
and deprived even of the religious element found in Platonism.
It is an altogether rational dialectic dealing with abstract
ideas. The problem is to find the proper name of God, which
will express His essence. All the names used to designate
God are either just signs, without any cognitive value, human
inventions κατ' ἐπίνοιαν, or else synonyms of the name
above all names which expresses perfectly what God is in
His essence. This objective name of God Eunomius finds in
the term ἀγέννητος—unbegotten, and in the concept ἀγεννησία—that which cannot be begotten. This is not a name
for the relationship which opposes the unbegotten Father to
the begotten Son. Nor is it a negative definition of what
God is not. For Eunomius ἀγεννησία has a positive meaning, that of being in itself, of self-sufficiency [asséité], to
use a scholastic term; i.e. a substance which exists by itself,
having the foundation of its being within itself, existing
within its own being. Thus the concept of ἀγεννησία gives
an adequate notion of the very essence of God, so much so
that it can be said that God knows nothing of His essence
that we do not know already ourselves.

The violent reaction against Eunomianism and the very
lively polemic against Eunomius, carried on especially by the

great Cappadocians, indicates to what extent the Fathers of the fourth century were aware of the danger of intellectualism in the knowledge of God.

* * *

St. Basil (330-79), in his attack on Eunomius, criticizes him first of all on the philosophical level for his theory of knowledge. He firmly rejects the distinction between essential names of objects and names invented by reflection, κατ' ἐπίνοιαν. All names with which we designate objects are found by way of reflection, but this does not mean that this reflection is sterile, that it does not correspond to any objective reality. A body appears simple to us at first sight, but reflection progressively reveals its scope, color, thickness, form, and still other properties. This permits us to form concepts, penetrating in this way into the complexity of objects, giving them names which express their qualities or their relations to other objects, even though we are never able to exhaust the content of a being in concepts. There always remains an unknown something, an existential depth— if this modern expression can be applied to the thought of St. Basil—something which escapes all intellectual analysis. This means that there is not a single object which can be known in its essence, in that which makes it what it is and not something else. It must not be thought that in denying the possibility of knowing the essence of things, St. Basil professed a pessimistic gnosiology. On the contrary, to the intellectualized and impoverished world of Eunomius he opposed an extremely rich world, a world inexhaustible for thought; to the passive revelation of essences impressed on the soul by God he opposed the activity of human knowledge and at the same time its objective character. We do perceive the actual properties of objects, even if the names by which we designate things do not really express what they are in essence.

If this is true for the knowledge of created beings, still less can the essential concept of divine reality be expressed in a concept. The names which we apply to God reveal to us a particular reality which we contemplate. But there is not one among all the divine names which expresses what God is in essence. The negative names tell us what God is not, forbidding the use of concepts alien to God. Other names indicate what must be conceived when we think of God. But both types of names are posterior to the divine reality, both come *after* God. This is even more true in that, contrary to knowledge of things involving only human activity, the knowledge of God implies also a revelatory action on God's part. All the divine names that we find in the Scriptures show us God as He reveals Himself to created beings.

God manifests Himself by His operations or energies. "While we affirm," says St. Basil, "that we know our God in his energies, we scarcely promise that he may be approached in his very essence. For although his energies descend to us, his essence remains inaccessible." This passage from the letter to Amphilochius[5] together with other texts in *Against Eunomius*[6] will have an importance of the very first order for the doctrine of the vision of God. Byzantine theologians will often quote this authority in formulating the distinction between the inaccessible οὐσία and its natural processions, the ἐνέργειαι or manifesting operations.

Eunomius also speaks of operations and calls them ἐνέργειαι.[7] But in his doctrine, where the transcendence of the οὐσία of the Father is connected with the absolute simplicity of the ἀγέννητος, all distinction becomes a separation, an opposition of created and uncreated natures. Also the ἐνέργεια of Eunomius is presented as a will or creative force conferred on the Son, the only being created immediately by

[5]Letter 234. PG. 32, col. 869.
[6]I, 6. PG. 29, cols. 521-4; II, 4, cols. 577-80; II, 32, col. 648.
[7]*Apologia*. PG. 30, col. 859.

the Father. This energy is by no means a manifestation of God; it is a created effect, a product of the Father in the Son who is "dissimilar" (ἀνόμοιος) to Him. We can notice here the Arian deformation of a concept in the theology of the first centuries which in regarding the Son as the manifestation of the Father often drifted towards subordinationism, making the Word an instrument of creation. The Fathers of the fourth century exalted the Trinity above every revelatory economy, made the Son into an *absolute* manifestation, a manifestation in Himself, addressed to no one, of the absolute reality of the divine Being; so then the external manifestation of God in created being had to be presented in post-Nicene theology as the energy of the unique οὐσία of the Trinity. This idea will find its doctrinal development later on. In St. Basil it is only adduced in order to affirm, against Eunomius, the objective character of the divine names κατ᾽ ἐπίνοιαν, by which we express a certain notion of God without ever comprehending His very essence.

But beside the names which designate the external manifestations of God, there are others which we apply to the interior relationships of the Trinity, to the being of God in Himself, without regard to acts of creation and providence. Through the Incarnation of the Word we can catch a glimpse of these relationships whose character transcends the natural faculties of our thought, and we examine them very imperfectly by using certain conceptual terms to suggest in relative language these absolute relationships, in which relationship itself is no longer relative. Thus trinitarian theology becomes theology *par excellence,* where speculation is inseparable from contemplation, where thought surpasses concepts without, however, forsaking its characteristic faculty of reflection or discernment. Origen had already distinguished θεολογία, or the knowledge of God in the Logos, from φυσικὴ θεωρία, the knowledge of creatures on the level of providence; i.e. from the manifestation of God in created beings. But while θεολογία was for Origen a contempla-

tion, a vision in the Logos of the abyss of the Father, for
Byzantine thought (as we shall see) it will designate
trinitarian speculation or the heritage of the Fathers of the
fourth century, as opposed to οἰκονομία, the relative lessons
of the external manifestations of God in created being, i.e.
the acts of creation, providence, redemption and sanctification.

Instead of contemplation of the οὐσία it is here knowledge of the Trinity which constitutes the object of theology.
Simplicity is no longer the dominating characteristic, since
by discerning the internal relationships of the divine being
reflection directs contemplation toward something which
surpasses the intelligible οὐσία or super-intelligible unity.
Also the gnosis of Clement and Origen yields to communion
with the Trinitarian God, a communion which is not expressed in terms of knowledge. Basil speaks of "intimacy
with God," of "union in love" (ἡ προσεδρεία τοῦ θεοῦ,
καὶ ἡ διὰ τῆς ἀγάπης συνάφεια).[8] Where Clement and
Origen spoke of gnosis, or deifying knowledge, St. Basil
will speak of the Holy Spirit. "God alone is God in essence.
By saying 'God alone' I am referring to the holy and uncreated essence of God." ... "Being God by nature, the Holy
Spirit deifies by grace those who still belong to a nature subjected to change."[9] "Through him the ascent of the emo-
tions, the deification of the weak, the fulfilment of that
which is in progress is accomplished. It is he who, shining
brightly in those who are being purified of all uncleanness,
makes them spiritual persons (πνευματικοὺς) through
communion with himself." It is in the Holy Spirit that we
can contemplate God: "As the sun when it falls on a pure
eye, the Holy Spirit will show you in himself the image of
the Invisible One. In the joyous contemplation of this image
you will see the ineffable beauty of the Archetype."[10] In the
Holy Spirit we see the image of the Son, and through Him

[8]*Hom. quod est Deus*, 6. PG. 31, col. 344B.
[9]*Contra Eun.*, III, 5. PG. 29, col. 665BC.
[10]*De Spiritu Sancto*, IX, 23. PG. 32, col. 109.

we see the Archetype, the Father. The whole vision of God
will be trinitarian: a vision in the Holy Spirit, through the
Son, directed toward the Father.

* * *

St. Gregory of Nazianzus (328-90), more than all the
others, spoke of the contemplation of the Trinity. Contrary
to his friend St. Basil, who remained a great administrator
even in theology, always inclined to concepts and seeking
to edify the Church by fixing in precise terms the path which
human thought should follow, St. Gregory of Nazianzus is
constantly drawn toward contemplation, even when he is
reasoning and debating. His writing is always an elevated
discourse, vibrating with deep emotion; often it is a rhythmic
chant, a meditative prayer in verse. At the end of his life
he wishes to be "where the Trinity is, where magnificence
is joined with splendor... the Trinity, whose merging
shadows alone fill me with emotion."[11] To see God is to
contemplate the Trinity while fully participating in His light.
"There will be heirs of the perfect light," he says, "and of
the contemplation of the most Holy and Sovereign Trinity...
those who will be wholly united to the whole Spirit. This
will be, as I believe, the celestial Kingdom."[12]

The divine magnificence which can be contemplated in
creation is only a little ray of that great light (μεγάλου
φωτὸς μικρὸν ἀπαύγασμα). No man has ever discovered
God as He is in His essence or nature, nor will ever discover
Him; or rather, we will discover God when the godlike image,
our spirit, is elevated to its Archetype and joined to that
with which it is familiar (τῷ οἰκείῳ προσμίξῃ), when
we know even as we are known.[13] This is the state of the
celestial Kingdom, the vision face to face, knowledge of the

[11]*Poems about himself*, 11. PG. 37, cols. 1165-7.
[12]*Or.* XXI, 9. PG. 35, col. 945c.
[13]*Or.* XXVIII, 2nd theol. PG. 36, cols. 48-9.

Trinity in the plenitude of His light. However, "the first
and most pure nature is known only by himself, i.e. by the
Holy Trinity."[14] The essence is "the Holy of Holies who
dwells hidden even from the Seraphim, being glorified by
the Three Sanctities united in one single Dominion and
Divinity."[15] In this world we converse with God "in a cloud"
like Moses, for God has set a darkness (σκότος) between
Himself and us; so then we are attracted all the more to the
light that is found with so much difficulty. He eludes our
sight more than He appears to us. But the last stone which
Moses comes upon already represents the humanity of Christ,
and the effulgence of light apparent in human form reveals
His divinity to the three apostles, by making plain what had
been concealed by the flesh.[16]

St. Gregory of Nyssa speaks often of the light, of the
illumination (φωτισμὸς) of the Trinity. The darkness, for
him, is something which must be overcome, as an obstruc-
tion to the light; it is not the condition of supreme knowledge, where knowledge becomes ignorance. But in spite of
this, and even though he says that the Kingdom of God is
the contemplation of the Trinity, union with God surpasses
gnosis: "If to know is already a beatitude, how much greater
is the One who is known?" "If it is so good to be subjected
to the Trinity, what will it be to have possession of Him?"[17]
The divine nature surpasses intelligence, and though they may
contemplate the Trinity, though they may receive the plenitude
of His light, human intellects (and even the angelic powers
close to God and illuminated by all His splendor) cannot
know God in His nature.[18]

It is difficult to clarify the doctrine of St. Gregory of
Nazianzus on the manner of the vision of God. Sometimes
he denies the possibility of knowing the divine essence, refus-

[14]ibid., col. 29AB.
[15]In Theophan. or. XXXVIII, 8. PG. 36, col. 320BC.
[16]Or. XXXII, 16. PG. 36, col. 193.
[17]Or. XIII, 11. PG. 35, col. 1164.
[18]Or. XXVIII, 4. PG. 36, col. 32.

ing this knowledge even to angels; sometimes he uses expressions which could lead us to think that the very nature of God can be known in the contemplation of the Trinity, in being "united" with or "merged" entirely in the entire Trinity. One fact remains certain: it is not here an intellectual contemplation tending toward the comprehension of a primary simplicity, toward the unity of a simple substance. Its object is "the three lights which form one single light," "the united refulgence" of the Trinity, the mystery of the Trinity hidden even to the seraphim.

As in the thought of St. Basil, so also with St. Gregory of Nazianzus the intellectualistic or super-intellectualistic mysticism of Alexandria is superseded. It is no longer the subordinationist Trinity of Origen so closely related to the thought of Plotinus, where one climbs from one step to the next in order to contemplate finally the abyss of the Father or, as with Plotinus, to be identified with the One. Thought reaches a mystery which surpasses any kind of primary unity: it distinguishes absolute relationships, without entirely comprehending the Trinity. "I did not begin to think of the Unity when the Trinity was bathing me in his splendor. I did not begin to think of the Trinity when the Unity possessed me. When one of the Three presents himself to me, I think that this is everything, so full is my eye, so much does all else escape my sight; for in my spirit, too limited to understand even the One, there is no longer room for any other. When I unite the Three in the same thought I see a single flame, without being able to divide or analyze this unified light."[19]

This is not a vision of God, nor is it, properly speaking, a speculation. It could be said that it is trinitarian speculation grafted on to contemplation, an intellectual revelation in the light which passes understanding. More than the two other Cappadocians, St. Gregory of Nazianzus received (through Didymus) the Alexandrian heritage. This is why

---

[19] *In sanctum baptisma, or.* 40, 41. PG. 36, col. 417.

the contemplation of the Trinity—which for him replaced
the vision of the οὐσία—is the central theme in his doctrine
of the vision of God, if indeed we can speak of a doctrine
when the nature of the vision is so little clarified.

*   *   *

St. Gregory of Nyssa (c. 335-99) took an active part in
the Eunomian controversy. This is illustrated by his twelve
books against Eunomius. Like his brother St. Basil, St. Gregory
of Nyssa asserts that we do not come to know essences, even
in created things. Our intellect discovers the properties of
things in the exact measure necessary for our life. If we
could know the grounds of things we would be dazzled by
the creative power which produces them. Our intellect is
always moving, discovering by reflection properties that are
still unknown; but the things in themselves remain inexhaustible for discursive knowledge. Words and names invented by thought are indispensable in establishing notions
of things in the memory, in enabling communication with
other human beings. The word loses all its value wherever
knowledge is stopped, where thought becomes contemplation. This is why "there is only one name for expressing the
divine nature—i.e. the wonder which seizes us when we
think of God."[20]

The common feature of all three Cappadocians is the
active role of thought, reflection or the faculty of discerning
as applied to the knowledge of God. St. Basil, being especially preoccupied with dogmatic questions, uses this faculty
to establish clear notions or landmarks for thought. St.
Gregory of Nazianzus transforms it into wondering contemplation of the ineffable relationships within God. St.
Gregory of Nyssa uses it to transcend the intelligible and
to find then a more sublime path to communion with God.

Like St. Basil, St. Gregory of Nyssa distinguishes between

[20]*In Cant. Cant.* XII. PG. 44, col. 1028.

the negative and positive names applied to God. The negative names, without revealing the divine nature to us, set aside everything that is alien to it. Even names which seem positive to us have, in reality, a negative meaning. Thus, in saying that God is good, we are declaring only that there is no room in Him for evil. The name "beginning" (ἀρχὴ) signifies that He Himself is without beginning. Other names, having a truly positive meaning, refer to the divine operations or energies; they lead us to know God not in His inaccessible essence but in what surrounds Him. "Wherefore it is true both that the pure heart sees God and that no one has ever seen God. In fact he who is invisible by nature becomes visible by his ἐνέργειαι, appearing to us in the particular surroundings of his nature" (ἐν τισι τοῖς περὶ αὐτὸν καθορωμένοις).[21]

In the same homily, devoted to the question of the vision of God (since the fourth Beatitude concerns the "pure in heart who will see God"), St. Gregory of Nyssa wonders if this contemplation of the divine attributes is sufficient to procure beatitude. Actually it is not sufficient simply to know the reason for sanctity; we must live in sanctity in order to be truly happy. In the same way beatitude does not consist in the fact that something is known about God, but in having Him within oneself (ἐν ἑαυτῷ σχεῖν τὸν θεόν). For St. Gregory of Nyssa this is in some way preferable to the face to face vision: "It is not the vision of God face to face (ἀντιπρόσωπόν τι θέαμα) which seems to me to be proposed here for the one whose soul's eye has been purified. What is proposed to us in this magnificent formula is perhaps what in clearer terms the Word expressed to some others when he said 'the Kingdom of Heaven is within you'; that we might learn that having purified our heart of all creatureliness and carnal disposition we will see the image of the divine nature in all its beauty. . . . Thus the mode of contemplation which is proper for you is that which looks

[21]*6th Homily on the Beatitudes*. PG. 44, col. 1269.

within. . . . Just as those who look at the sun in a mirror, even
though they cannot gaze at the sky itself, see the sun in the shining of the mirror no less than those who look at the solar disc
itself; so too if you have been dazzled by the light (of God),
in so far as you recover the grace of the image deposited in
you at the beginning, you possess what you seek within you.
Divinity is in fact purity, impassibility, the removal of all
evil. If this is what you are within, then God is within. When
your spirit is untainted by any evil, free from passions, separated from all uncleanness, you are blessed with clearness of
sight. Being purified, you know what is invisible to the
impure. The carnal fog having been raised from the eyes
of your soul, in the clear air (αἰθρία) of the heart you
contemplate the glorious spectacle (τὸ μακάριον θέαμα)
as far as the eye can see."[22]

Fr. Daniélou notes that this expression (τὸ μακάριον
θέαμα) recalls the passage in *Phaedrus* where the souls
passing about the canopy of heaven enjoy the spectacle of
the beatific vision (μακάριον ὄψιν καὶ θέαν). For Fr.
Danielou this interiorization of the θεωρία, which according
to St. Gregory of Nyssa is disclosed in the purified heart
or mirror of the soul, marks a complete reversal of the
Platonic perspective. Intellectual θεωρία, the Platonic
νοητά, is no longer for Gregory the summit of the ascent to
the divine. It is a summit only in relation to the created
world. In Platonic writings (and to some extent in Origen)
the κόσμος νοητός actually belongs to the sphere of the
divine; it was co-natural with God for Clement and Origen,
something opposed to the sensible world. For St. Gregory
of Nyssa, on the contrary, the line of demarcation passes
directly between the created world (sensible and intelligible)
and the divine Being. Thus the sensible and intelligible
cosmos is reassembled within the soul which contemplates
in its purified image (as in a mirror) the deifying energies.
First to participate in these deifying energies are intelligible

[22]ibid., col. 1272BC.

creatures, i.e. the angels—pure images, to whom the soul is enlikened. Thus the celestial journey of the soul (a common theme in all Platonic writings) is interiorized, there is an interior ascent: the soul finds its native land—what is co-natural with itself—within itself, by recovering its primitive state. This is the summit of θεωρία, of vision. But God remains unknown in Himself, incomprehensible in His nature. In his Commentary on the Song of Songs, St. Gregory of Nyssa shows us the soul in quest of its Beloved: "It rises afresh and in the spirit passes through the intelligible and hypercosmic world, which it calls the city, where there are Principalities, Dominions and Thrones assigned to Powers, it passes through the assembly of celestial beings, which it calls the public square, and their innumerable multitudes, which it calls the way, looking to see if its Beloved is among them. In its quest it passes through the whole angelic world and as it does not find the One it seeks among the blessed ones it encounters, it says to itself: 'Can any of these at least comprehend the One whom I love?' But they hold their tongues at this question, and by their silence make it realize that the One whom it seeks is inaccessible even to them. Then, having by the action of the spirit passed through the whole of the hypercosmic city, having failed to recognize the One it desires among intelligible and incorporeal beings, and abandoning all that it finds, it recognizes the One it is seeking as the only One he does not comprehend."[23]

In his sixth Homily on the Beatitudes, St. Gregory of Nyssa asks himself how eternal life can be promised to the pure in heart in the form of a vision of God if the vision of the divine essence is impossible. If God is life, he who does not see God will not see life. He refers to various texts of Scripture where "to see" has the meaning of "to possess" or "to have." Not to see something means not to share or participate in it. Thus, a new path is opened up beyond θεωρία, beyond vision, for the soul entering the darkness.

[23]PG. 44, col. 893.

As we have seen, darkness (γνόφος, σκότος) for St. Gregory of Nazianzus is that which separates us from the light of the Trinity. For St. Gregory of Nyssa, on the contrary, the darkness through which Moses penetrated to the summit of Sinai represents a form of communion with God, superior to the contemplation of the light of the burning bush in which God appeared to Moses at the beginning of his wanderings. This is why, as he develops the doctrine of spiritual senses which he finds in Origen's thought, St. Gregory of Nyssa pays less attention to sight, "the most intellectual sense," as Fr. Daniélou remarks.

If God appears as light and then as darkness, this means— for Gregory—that there is no vision of the divine essence and that union is presented as a path which goes beyond vision, θεωρία, beyond intelligence, to the area where knowledge is suppressed and love alone remains, or rather where gnosis becomes *agape:* ἡ δὲ γνῶσις ἀγάπη γίνεται. Desiring God more and more, the soul does not cease to grow and pass beyond itself, to depart out of itself, and its love becomes more ardent and insatiable to the extent that it is united more and more with God. Thus the bride of the Song of Songs awaits her Bridegroom with the awareness that the union will have no end, that the ascent to God has no termination, that beatitude is an infinite progression. . . .

Our exposition of the doctrine of the vision of God in the writings of St. Gregory of Nyssa would be incomplete if we did not take note of still another point on which Fr. Daniélou insists in his book.[24] This is the inhabitation of the soul by the Word, the mystical experience which is one sign of developing consciousness: the experience through the spiritual senses of the presence of Christ within, i.e. an entering within oneself—plus an ecstatic experience, a going out from oneself, in the tension of love, directed toward the Word as He is in Himself, i.e. toward the incomprehensible nature of God.

[24]*Platonisme et théologie mystique,* Paris, 1944.

The thought of the Fathers of the fourth century marks a decisive step in the Christian transformation of the Alexandrian Hellenism of Clement and Origen. This is especially evident on the purely dogmatic level, where the Trinity no longer leaves room for a simple, monistic God, an intelligible or supra-intelligible substance and the source of spiritual being. In St. Gregory of Nyssa we see to what extent this overcoming of Platonic concepts is carried out simultaneously on the level of spirituality. Here, however, Origen's influence will be more tenacious and will make itself felt for a long time, through the agency of Evagrius of Pontus, who will introduce the intellectual gnosis of Origen into the closed world of Christian ascetics and monks. But before examining the question of the vision of God in the ascetic and spiritual tradition, we must glance briefly at the theology of vision in the works of other Fathers of the fourth and fifth centuries, in order to reach in this way, through Dionysius the Areopagite, what can be properly called the world of Byzantine thought.

CHAPTER FIVE

The Syro-Palestinians
and Saint Cyril of Alexandria

In speaking of the reaction against Eunomius' rationalism
in the doctrine of the knowledge of God, we have dwelt
especially on the three great Cappadocians, St. Basil, St.
Gregory of Nyssa and St. Gregory of Nazianzus. Cappadocia,
in the fourth century, was a focal point of theological thought,
in which the great task of Christianizing the philosophical
technique of the Greek world was being consciously pursued.
The mystical intellectualism of Alexandria will be superseded and transformed in the doctrinal synthesis crowned
by the dogma of the Trinity. The gnosis of Clement and
Origen will be reduced to a subordinate function: *theology*—
the contemplation of God—will no longer lead to a spirituality
of escape, of return to God through the intellect; it will be
presented as but one of several necessary elements in the
communion with the God-Trinity.

If Hellenistic traces are still to be seen in the writings of
the Christians of Alexandria (a Synesius, for example, is
more indebted to Platonism than was Origen), there are in
the fourth century other theological spheres which remained
alien to the whole drift of Greek intellectualism. There is,
first of all, the world of Syrian spirituality: Aphraates and
St. Ephraim of Syria. Biblical connections are most strong

in the latter's writing. The apophatic moment is dominant
when he speaks of God, and there is an accent of religious
dread. Aware of the infinite distance which separates the
creature from the Creator, he refuses to seek a knowledge
of God, for the Inaccessible One is by nature dreadful. St.
Ephraim violently opposes the "scrutinizers," the Eunomian
rationalists; he wishes that there no longer be a search for
mystical gifts or representation of the contemplation of
God as the goal of the Christian life. The Church occupies
a large part of his theological thought; the Church as the
context of sanctification, where union with God is realized
in the sacraments.

Among theologians writing in Greek in Syria and Palestine
St. Cyril of Jerusalem (315-86) develops in particular this
sacramental aspect of the contemplation of God. He speaks
of the vision of God more in negative terms: only the Son
and the Holy Spirit have a pure vision (ἀκραιφνὲς εἰλι-
κρινῶς) of the nature of the Father, in which they participate fully. In fact it is said that only the Son sees the
Father and that the Holy Spirit searches the depths (τὰ
βάθη) of God. It is with and by the Holy Spirit (σὺν τῷ
Πνεύματι, διὰ τοῦ Πνεύματος τοῦ ἁγίου) that the
Son reveals the Divinity to the angels in a measure appropriate to their ranks (κατὰ τὸ μέτρον τῆς οἰκείας
τάξεως), according to the faculty (δύναμιν) of each
one. Although the angels of children always contemplate the
face of the Father they do not see God as He is, but only
in so far as they can grasp and contain Him (ἀλλὰ βλέ-
πουσιν οἱ ἄγγελοι οὐ καθώς ἐστιν ὁ θεός, ἀλλὰ
καθόσον αὐτοὶ χωροῦσιν). If it is like this for angels,
men should not be upset by their ignorance. We can know
only that much of God which human nature can grasp
(κεχώρηκεν), only as much as our human frailty (ἀσθέ-
νεια) can support. For those who are near God, the greatest
knowledge is the knowledge of their own ignorance ('Εν

τοῖς γὰρ περὶ θεοῦ, μεγάλη γνῶσις τὸ τὴν ἀγνωσίαν ὁμολογεῖν).[1]

*   *   *

St. Epiphanius of Cyprus (315-413) dealt with the question of the vision of God in his *Panarion* or "Box of Remedies"[2] for heresies. If while refusing to man the possibility of seeing God the Scriptures also affirm this vision, it is because God, unknowable by nature, makes Himself seen, shows Himself, out of His own good will. He is seen not as the Infinite (ἄπειρος) but as He who manifests Himself to us by adapting the mode of revelation to our faculty of perception. To see the sky through a crack in the roof—is to see the sky, but also not to see it. In the Incarnation, the Son clothed in flesh is made known to men; but as God He surpasses our faculty of comprehension. Nevertheless all that we can say of Him is true.

St. John Chrysostom (344-407) reacted against Eunomius in his twelve homilies *On the Incomprehensible Nature of God.* He also dealt with the question of the vision of God in his fifteenth homily on the Gospel of St. John, in which he expounded the words "No one has ever seen God." God's nature, simple, without form, without composition (ἁπλῆ, ἀσχημάτιστος, ἀσύνθετος), is never an object of vision. If Isaiah, Ezekiel and other prophets had truly seen the very essence of God, it would have appeared the same for all. God says to Hosea: "I have multiplied visions and have likened myself in the hands of the prophets" (Hos. 12: 19). This means: "I have not revealed my very essence, but (in visions) I condescend to the frailty of those who see me."[3] All that can be seen of God pertains to His condescension and not to the vision of His pure essence (ὅτι πάντα ἐκεῖ- να συγκαταβάσεως ἦν, οὐκ αὐτῆς τῆς οὐσίας γυ-

---

[1] *Catechism VI,* 2. PG. 33, col. 540; cf. *Catech. VII,* 11; ibid., col. 617.
[2] LXX, 7 and 8. PG. 42, cols. 349-53.
[3] *On the Incomprehensibility of God,* V, 4. PG. 48, col. 740.

μνῆς ὄψις).[4] What is this condescension (συγκατάβασις)? It is the manifestation of God as He makes Himself
visible "not as he is, but as he who sees him is capable of
seeing, by proportioning the vision to the poverty (ἀσθέ-
νεια) of those who are seeing."[5] This is true not only for
men who know Him in this world "in part," "in a mirror
and in riddles," but also for angels who have a vision of
God face to face. Even the perfect vision is adapted to the
perceptivity of the creature; even in heaven God reveals
Himself in condescension and the angelic powers avert their
eyes, unable to bear this revelatory descent (συγκατάβα-
σιν) of God.[6] What vision (ὅρασις) is for us knowledge
(γνῶσις) is for incorporeal spirits. However, neither angels
nor archangels know the essence of God. They do not even
seek to know, like Eunomius, what God is in His essence,
but rather ceaselessly glorify and adore Him.[7]

This condescension or economy of God who is by nature
inaccessible corresponds, in St. John Chrysostom, to the
revelatory operations or energies coming down to us which
we encountered in St. Basil and St. Gregory of Nyssa. A
moralist rather than a theologian, Chrysostom gave a psy-
chological nuance to these manifestations of God, to His
departure out of His essence. We have here a merciful will
which descends to the inferior state of created beings. For
St. Chrysostom this compassionate descent ends finally in
the Incarnation of the Son. Being the perfect image of the
Invisible God, the Son is Himself invisible: otherwise He
would not be the image of the Father. By manifesting Himself in the flesh He became visible also to the angels. It is
in this way that Chrysostom interprets the words of St. Paul
(1 Tim. 3: 16): "God appeared in the flesh, ... has shown
himself to the angels." Before the Incarnation or descent of
the Son to created beings the angels saw God only in their

[4]*On St. John* 15, 1. PG. 59, col. 98.
[5]*On the Incomp.*, III, 3. PG. 48, col. 722.
[6]ibid., I, 6, col. 707.
[7]*On St. John* 15, 1. PG. 59, col. 98.

thought (κατὰ διάνοιαν ὄψις), by imagining (φαντά-
ζονται) Him in their pure and vigilant natures.[8] Thus the
vision of God is conditioned, for created beings, by His
Incarnation: the perfect expression of His condescension, a
hypostatic συγκατάβασις. The Son alone has that knowledge of God which is a perfect *theoria* or κατάληψις
(comprehension), for He is in the bosom of the Father.
He has revealed God to us. Chrysostom has in mind St.
John's term: ἐξηγήσατο in its proper meaning, i.e. to
explain, to interpret, to tell about. By His miracles, His
example and His teaching, Christ has revealed God to us
and this revelation has in particular a moral character. While
revealing God in His incarnation, the Son ("the invisible
image") remains hidden in His divinity. Even in the Transfiguration He permits the appearance only of a light that
is adapted to mortal sight; once more it is a vision "in a
mirror and in a riddle," "an obscure image of future
blessings,"[9] of the divine glory of Christ which will be contemplated by immortal eyes in eternal life.

So then to summarize St. John Chrysostom's thought on
the vision of God, we may say that God, invisible and unknowable in His essence, makes Himself known and appears by going out of His own nature, so to speak, and
descending to created beings, and that this condescension
(συγκατάβασις), as the work of His will, is the Incarnation of the Son, by which the Word as the invisible image
of God becomes visible to angels as well as to men. In the
age to come Christ will be seen clothed in divine glory and
this will be the vision of God "face to face." God has
manifested Himself by becoming man, this is why God will
be seen in the humanity of Christ.

This view is common to the whole school of Antioch,
whose studious piety is attracted to the concrete person of
the Christ of the Gospel. More accentuated in the thought

---

[8]ibid., 15, 2. PG. 59, col. 100.
[9]*Ad Theod. laps.*, 1, 11. PG. 61, col. 292.

of Theodore of Mopsuestia and Theodoret, the fathers of
Nestorianism, this view will reduce the vision of God simply
to the perception of the human nature of Christ. If for St.
John Chrysostom the person of the Son was the "invisible
image" becoming visible in the Incarnation, for Theodore of
Mopsuestia (350-428) it is only the man Jesus who is the
image of the invisible divinity."[10]

*   *   *

Theodoret of Cyrrhus (393-453) in his dialogues "The
Mendicant, or The Mutable," known also under the title
"On Immutability," while defending the immutability of
the divine Word in the Incarnation, affirms the absolute
invisibility of God, even to angels.[11] Created beings (men
and angels) can see God only in revelations proportionate
to their faculties of perception, in "likenesses" which do not
reveal the very nature of God—just as the effigies of em-
perors on coins are only remote likenesses.[12] Angels, as they
behold the face of the Father, do not see the divine, infinite
(ἀπερίγραπτον), incomprehensible (ἀπερίληπτον), un-
thinkable (ἀπερινόητον), all-embracing (περιληπτικὴν
τῶν ὅλων) essence, but only a particular glory in proportion to their nature (ἀλλὰ δόξαν τινὰ τῇ αὐτῶν φύσει
συμμετρουμένην).[13] What is the nature of this glory?
Probably, for Theodoret, it is not by divine energies that
God manifests His presence but by a created effect, for he
prefers to use the scriptural expression "the likeness of
glory." In the Incarnation God has appeared to angels and
also to men no longer in "the likeness of glory" but by
using true, living human flesh "like a disguise."[14] Invisible
nature was expressed through visible nature, performing

---

[10]*In Col.* I, 15. PG. 66, col. 928BC.
[11]PG. 83, col. 45.
[12]ibid., col. 49.
[13]ibid., col. 52.
[14]ibid.

miracles, revealing in this way the power which belongs to it (τὴν οἰκείαν δύναμιν). What is this visible nature? Theodoret tells us: the divine nature is invisible, but the flesh is visible.[15] The Lord revealed the δύναμις of His divine nature by His miracles. We have here the Nestorian parallelism: the divine person of the Son remains hidden in the humanity of Jesus. The body of Christ became invisible after the Ascension, but it can be perceived in symbols, in the Sacraments.[16] In the age to come the Lord Himself will be seen face to face, or rather, "both the faithful and the unfaithful will see the nature that he has taken from us, adored by all creation."[17] This is a vision of Christ's humanity, and nothing more. His divinity remains hidden. All dynamic motion, all "perichoresis" is alien to this theological thought which, in accentuating the concrete character of the vision of God in the human Christ, in pushing the tendencies of the Antiochene school to the extreme, completely rejects the vision of God properly so called, i.e. rejects any immediate communion with God and all possibility of the deification of created beings in the true sense of the word. There is an abuse here which is obviously just the opposite of the one we noticed in the Alexandrian school, in the writing of Clement and Origen, where intellectual gnosis or the contemplation of the divine essence replaces the personal encounter with Christ and intimate communion with the living God.

* * *

In the fifth century Alexandrian theology finds its most perfect and most orthodox expression in the thought of St. Cyril of Alexandria (370-444), dominated by the idea of deification as the supreme goal of created beings. The

[15]ibid., col. 48.
[16]*In 1 Cor.* XIII. PG. 82, cols. 336-7.
[17]*In Eph.* 2. PG. 82, col. 521.

tradition of St. Athanasius is enriched here by the theological contributions of the three great Cappadocians, i.e. it is the Alexandrian theology of deification freed from every trace of Origenism and its spiritualistic ideal of escape through contemplation.

It is pure theology, a theology of the Holy Trinity, where there is no room whatsoever for the God of the philosophers, the ἕv of neo-Platonism, the spiritual monad. For St. Cyril the name Father is superior to that of God. "He is called Father," he says, "by the One who is best and most worthy, i.e. by the Son. He is called God by slaves, by those who are least; so great is the distance between the Master and the slave, between the Creator and the creature. Just as the word Father is related to the Son, so the word God is related to slaves and those who do not have the same nature as God, whatever that nature may be."[18] All created nature, spiritual or corporeal, is equally alienated from the un-created nature of God. However, according to the word of St. Peter all are called to become "partakers of the divine nature." Only the Word is the Son by nature, but by the fact of the Incarnation we become "sons by participation" (μέθεξις). To participate in the divinity of the Son, in the communal divinity of the Trinity, is to be deified, to be penetrated by divinity—just as the red-hot iron in the fire is penetrated by the heat of the fire—allowing the beauty of the inexpressible nature of the Trinity to shine in us.[19] We are deified by the Holy Spirit who makes us likenesses of the Son, the perfect image of the Father.[20] We become like the Son—"sons by participation"—by participating in the divine nature, by being united to God in the Holy Spirit.[21] We are deified by the Son in the Holy Spirit. "If (which is most im-probable) it should happen that we were to live deprived of the Spirit, we would not even suspect that God was in

[18]Relic 5. PG. 75, cols. 65-8.
[19]ibid., col. 189B.
[20]On St. John. PG. 74, col. 541.
[21]Relic 34, op. cit., col. 598.

us."[22] Not only does the Holy Spirit become the source of spiritual life in the soul, but He is also the principle of gnosis which makes us conscious of this life in grace. We see here how the intellectualistic gnosis of Clement and Origen is transformed in Alexandrian theology, losing all contact with Platonic contemplation.

The perfect knowledge of God which is attained in the age to come is no longer the ultimate goal, but one aspect of the final deification or of "the spiritual world of delights" (τρυφῆς δὲ τρόπος πνευματικός), as St. Cyril says. We shall know Christ who will shine in us by the Holy Spirit, because we shall have "the mind of Christ" (νοῦς Χριστοῦ) of which St. Paul spoke, and this mind of Christ is the Holy Spirit present in us.[23] Progressive deification, accompanied by an ever more perfect knowledge of God, is accomplished in the sacramental life. "Perfect gnosis of Christ," says St. Cyril, "is obtained by baptism and the illumination of the Holy Spirit."[24] The body takes part in this life in union with God, especially in the sacrament of the Eucharist, the corporeal union with Christ.[25]

The "divine darkness" or knowledge through ignorance has no place in the thought of St. Cyril. Like St. Gregory of Nazianzus he often speaks of illumination (φωτισμὸς) and if knowledge is superseded in the age to come, this means for him that partial knowledge—"in riddles and in a mirror"—will be eclipsed there by the illumination of Christ which will fill our minds with divine and ineffable light (θείου τινὸς καὶ ἀπορρήτου φωτός).[26] "'We shall see God as he is.' This means that with uncovered face and untrammelled thought we shall have in our intellect (ἐννοήσομεν) the beauty of the divine nature of the Father, while contemplating the glory of the One who has shone

[22]*On St. John*, op. cit., col. 545A.
[23]ibid., cols. 284-5.
[24]*On Ex.* II. PG. 69, col. 432A.
[25]*On St. John* VI, 54. PG. 73, cols. 577B-8A.
[26]*On Malach.* IV, 2-3. PG. 72, col. 360AC.

forth from him" (τὴν τοῦ πεφηνότος ἐξ αὐτοῦ θεω-
ρήσαντες δόξαν).[27]

This is a very important text for the doctrine of the
vision of God face to face. As in St. Irenaeus, and as
with the theologians of the school of Antioch, it has reference to Christ. But it is not simply His human nature
(as in Theodoret) but the divine and incarnated person
who makes visible in His own glory what is also the glory
of the Father, the "beauty (κάλλος) of the divine nature"[28]
in which we participate through the Holy Spirit. And St.
Cyril quotes the word of St. Paul (2 Cor. 5: 16): "If we
have known Christ according to the flesh, we know him in
this way no more." Christ's glory shines in those who have
acquired divine intelligence (θεία σύνεσις), for they are
inflamed by the same Spirit who deified the human nature
of the Son. It is indeed Christ whom we see face to face,
but this vision is inseparable from communion with the whole
Trinity in the illumination of the age to come.

The theologians of Byzantium will receive the heritage
of two schools, the school of Antioch, especially through
St. John Chrysostom, and the school of Alexandria through
St. Cyril. If the first current in the doctrine of the vision
of God involves a certain limitation, since it is connected
especially with the person of Christ as revealed in His humanity, the second current places emphasis on "the beauty
of the divine nature," on the eternal glory of Christ which
He shares with the Father and the Holy Spirit. The thought
of Antioch follows the movement of divine condescension,
which adapts the manifestation of God to the faculties of
created beings; it is above all Christological. The thought of
Alexandria follows the opposite movement—that of man
being raised to union with God, to deification; it is a school
of thought that is conspicuous for its pneumatological
emphasis.

[27]*On St. John* XVI, 25. PG. 73, col. 464B.
[28]ibid.

Some scholars have noted a decline after the middle of the fifth century in the great theological literature of the East. "The names of Theodoret and St. Cyril seem to close the list of the great writers of the Greek Church: the literary vein is exhausted, and there begins the age of a less eloquent but more subtle theology."[29] This is correct only from the purely literary point of view. The grand eloquence is ended, but great theological thought continues to develop. With Dionysius the Areopagite and St. Maximus we enter the world of truly Byzantine theology. But before approaching the doctrine of the vision of God in the *Corpus dionysiacum,* we must turn back and see how this question was raised among ascetic writers prior to the fifth century.

---

[29]Tixeront, *Histoire des dogmes,* Vol. 3, p. 4.

CHAPTER SIX

The Vision of God in Ascetic Literature

We shall now examine the question of the vision of God in a totally different light, i.e. as it is raised in ascetic literature. We shall turn back to the beginning of the fourth century, the period of the birth of monasticism.

While speaking of Origen we noticed how much more precise, more concrete, more full of life was his ideal of the contemplative life than that of Clement of Alexandria. Clement's gnostic man is a literary fiction. Origen's spiritual man, in spite of his kinship with the Platonic contemplatives, more closely approaches the type of the Christian ascetic. His Platonic spirituality of escape, of flight from the world and return to God by way of contemplation, is on the way to becoming a discipline of salvation, a Christian asceticism. However, the intellectualistic mysticism of Alexandria had no hold on the first generations of the great ascetics in Egypt. There is no trace in the life of St. Anthony, written by St. Athanasius, of the contemplative way as exalted above the way of action, or of contemplation as the Christian's goal. It is rather a way of continual prayer and watching, a life of practical virtues, a struggle for incorruptibility in which the human will heroically resists the cunning onslaughts of demons while striving to follow the commandments of the Gospel, above all the commandment to love God and one's neighbor.

103

It is this spirituality of struggle for incorruptibility (ἀφθαρσία) which St. Basil had in mind when he drew up his monastic regulations. In the monastic institution of communal or cenobitic (κοινὸς βίος) life he saw an ideal Christian community, a church within the Church, where the bonds of love broken apart in the world must be drawn together again, where a life in the image of the Holy Trinity must be realized on earth in the renunciation of one's own will in obedience, in uniting with one's brothers on the common path of union with God. The vision of God; contemplation—as the goal for a monk; the pursuit of the mystical gifts; gnosis; none of these have any place in this cenobitic spirituality. We can easily understand why the monk Evagrius, an assiduous reader of Origen, abandoned a community of this type "out of love for philosophy and divine truth," as he himself put it.

* * *

Evagrius of Pontus, born *c.* 345, was made a reader by St. Basil; St. Gregory of Nyssa ordained him deacon, and he accompanied St. Gregory of Nazianzus to Constantinople in 380. But in spite of his close relations with the three great Cappadocians, in particular with St. Gregory of Nazianzus, whom he considered as his teacher, Evagrius formulated his thought mainly from his reading of Origen. He came to Egypt in 383 and entered a monastery in Nitria, but left it at once to find a more suitable place for the contemplative life in the desert of Scete, to the west of the delta. In this "desert of cells" (organized by St. Macarius, a disciple of St. Anthony) he tried to realize the ideal of contemplative life outlined by Origen. Evagrius died in 399, having gained a reputation as a great master of the spiritual life. He left several writings which are manuals of spirituality in which Origen's ideas on Christian perfection, adapted for the use of monks, are set forth in the concise and clear fashion of ascetical and mystical maxims. Evagrius has the honor of introducing into ascetical literature the literary form of "annals" [trans: centuries], collections of a hundred chapters or definitions. But it is also through him that Origen's intellectualism, overcome on the dogmatic level, made its way into the realm of spirituality, giving a new richness to Christian asceticism and also creating new difficulties for it. It is Origen's strange destiny always to be attacked and at the same time to enrich those who are fighting against his thought. St. Jerome was the first to accuse Evagrius of Origenism. Evagrius will be condemned 150 years later, at the time of the fifth Council, together with Origen. Nevertheless his writings, translated into Syriac, Coptic and Latin, will continue to circulate among monks, sometimes under the name of St. Basil, or St. Nilus of Sinai. St. Maximus and others will make use of Evagrius without identifying him, aware of the riches contained in his teaching in spite of his Hellenistic defect, i.e. his intellectualistic mysticism. In our own day we are coming to see more and more clearly the major role played by Evagrius in the history of Christian spirituality. His literary heritage has increased prodigiously through the discovery of other texts known hitherto under false names.

Evagrius' works fall into three groups, corresponding to the three stages of the Christian life established by Origen: the active life, the struggle for ἀπάθεια; gnosis, or the contemplation of sensible and intelligible nature; and θεολογία, divine gnosis, according to Origen the contemplation of the divine nature, or, according to Evagrius, the contemplation of the Trinity. Evagrius will give the name prayer (προσευχή) to this last and supreme stage.

Asceticism really corresponds to the πρακτική; this first stage on the way to perfection involves a scale of virtues beginning with the lowest step—faith, and coming next to fear of God, the observance of the commandments, temperance, prudence, patience and hope. The summit of the

active life is ἀπάθεια, impassibility or, rather, the state in
which one is no longer disturbed by passions. The fruit of
ἀπάθεια is love—the crown of asceticism. It may be recalled
that with Origen too love was the "doorway to gnosis."
Evagrius goes further still, declaring: "Only love of the good
lives for ever (an allusion to St. Paul's passage on ἀγάπη).
This is the love of true knowledge" (...τῆς ἀληθείας
γνώσεως ἀγάπη).[1] This definition of love has a strong
intellectualistic accent: the perfect love which never dies is
love of divine gnosis. Elsewhere Evagrius says, in the same
spirit: "Love is the lofty state (ὑπερβάλλουσα κατάστα-
σις) of the rational soul by virtue of which it is able to
love nothing in this world so much as the knowledge of
God."[2] But before coming to the contemplation of God or
spiritual gnosis (γνῶσις πνευματική), the intellect must
be trained for the knowledge of God in creation, for physical
gnosis or θεωρία, the gnosis of sensible and intelligible
natures. We have here an arena for exercise, a gymnasium
of the intellect where, once delivered from passions through
πρακτική, it is trained for contemplation before seeing
God. This is also the "kingdom of heaven," as Evagrius
says: "The kingdom of heaven is the impassibility of the
soul united with the true contemplation of beings." But it is
not yet the Kingdom of God, which is the contemplation
of the Holy Trinity.[3]

The contemplation of the Holy Trinity is the beginning
of gnosis; it is *theologia* (Origen used the same term to
designate the ultimate degree of perfection). It is also
prayer (προσευχὴ) or "pure prayer." For Evagrius theology,
gnosis of the Trinity and prayer are therefore synonymous.
"If you are a theologian," he says, "you will pray truly, and
if you pray truly, you are a theologian."[4] 'Απάθεια is not
sufficient for true prayer, since one can still be held back

[1]*Cent.* IV, 50. Ed. W. Frankenberg, p. 293.
[2]*Cent.* I, 86. Frankenberg, p. 123.
[3]*Cap. Practica*, 2 and 3. PG. 40, col. 1221.
[4]*Treatise on Prayer*, 60. Trans. I. Hausherr, RAM No. 57, p. 90.

by "simple thoughts," thoughts which are void of passion
but which obstruct the intellect.[5] All that informs the intellect—the νοῦς—carries it away from God. In the gnosis of
intelligible beings one is still held back by their multiplicity.
Therefore the purification begun in πρακτική, where the
ascetic triumphs over passions by means of virtue, must end
in gnosis. Virtue, says Evagrius, is nothing but a thought born
out of the passion which resists it. The gnostic man or "seer"
must pursue this purification by ridding himself of images
by way of spiritual knowledge. In the ultimate stage he will
be delivered from simple thoughts by prayer.[6] "Seek the
kingdom of heaven and its righteousness, and all the rest
will be added to you." Righteousness means here, for
Evagrius, the virtues of the active life; the kingdom of
heaven means the gnosis of beings. We must seek first
these virtues and this gnosis, and then the contemplation of
the Holy Trinity—the Kingdom of God—will be added in
the final state of prayer, no longer dependent on our will.

What is this state of prayer? It is "an impassible *habitus*
which through supreme love carries off to the summits of
intellect the spiritual mind (νοῦς) enamoured by wisdom."[7]
It is an "ascent of the intellect" toward God.[8] Again, "prayer
without distraction is the highest intellection of the mind."[9]
It is therefore in a state of intellectual contemplation that the
νοῦς acquires perfection. But Evagrius says elsewhere: "The
sinful soul (ψυχή) is the intellect (νοῦς) fallen from the
contemplation of the Monad."[10] We are here in the presence
of a completely Origenistic concept. As with Origen, so
with Evagrius ψυχή is a deformation of the νοῦς alienated
from God and materialized. It becomes spirit (νοῦς) again
by way of contemplation, whose perfect phase is pure prayer.

[5]ibid., 55-7. Hausherr, p. 86.
[6]*Cent.* VII, 26. Frankenberg, p. 481.
[7]*Treatise on Prayer,* 52. Hausherr, p. 84.
[8]ibid., 35, p. 70.
[9]ibid., 34ᵃ, p. 70.
[10]*Cent.* III, 28. Frankenberg, p. 207.

In the state of pure prayer the νοῦς becomes absolutely simple, "bare" (γυμνός). Even pure thoughts must be driven away from the mind, and this last perfection is a gift of God.[11] In this state, during prayer, the light of the Trinity shines in the spirit of the purified man. This state of νοῦς or intelligence is the summit of intelligible natures where they are (like heaven itself) filled with the light of the Trinity.[12] Prayer can be compared to vision; just as sight is the best of all the senses, so prayer is more divine than all the virtues.[13] But here "the name sight is given to what is accomplished by the intellectual sense."[14] It is thought which, during prayer, sees the light of the Holy Trinity (διά- νοια . . . καιρῷ προσευχῆς τὸ τῆς ἁγίας τριάδος φῶς βλέπουσα).[15] In the state of pure prayer the νοῦς becomes the place of God (τόπος Θεοῦ), the image of God the temple, the divine spirit, God by grace. In contemplating God the human mind understands itself, sees itself in seeing Him. The perception is simultaneous: by knowing God the νοῦς knows itself, as the place of God, as a receptacle of the light of the Trinity; and so it sees itself as clearly as one sees a sapphire or the sky. It is bare intellect (νοῦς γυμνός), "consummated in the vision of itself, having merited communion in the contemplation of the Holy Trinity."[16]

This doctrine, formulated in a way quite unlike Origen, can be linked rather with the θεωρία of St. Gregory of Nyssa, where God is contemplated in the mirror of the soul. However, for Evagrius this vision of the light of God in the deified νοῦς is the summit, the end which admits no transcendence. As with Origen, there is no ecstasy, no de- parting out of the self "above the νοῦς"; there is no longer

[11]*Cent.* V, 79. Frankenberg, p. 355.
[12]*Cent.* VII. Frankenberg, p. 425.
[13]*Treatise on Prayer*, 150. Hausherr, RAM No. 58, p. 166.
[14]*Cent.* VI, 56.
[15]*Anti-rhetoric*, p. 475.
[16]*Cent.* III, 6. Frankenberg, p. 193.

any divine darkness or knowledge through ignorance. We are aware of only one passage where Evagrius writes: "Blessed is the one who has descended into infinite ignorance" (Μακάριος ὁ φθάσας εἰς τὴν ἀπέραντον ἀγνωσίαν).[17] The word φθάσας—descended—would be surprising if it referred to an ecstatic state superior to the contemplation of the light of the Trinity in the soul. Actually, as Fr. Hausherr has shown, Evagrius means by the ἀπέραντος ἀγνωσία—infinite ignorance—the exclusion of all knowledge other than that of God. The bare intellect contemplating the Trinity becomes infinitely ignorant with respect to all that is inferior to the divine gnosis. We may recall St. Gregory of Nazianzus, whom Evagrius often called his teacher. For him the darkness of Sinai, which Moses entered in order to meet God, no longer had the meaning of a mode of communion with God superior to θεωρία. Γνόφος, for St. Gregory of Nazianzus, is the ignorance of the multitude concerning God; light is superior to darkness. St. Gregory of Nazianzus, who speaks a great deal of the contemplation of the Trinity, did not develop a doctrine of contemplation. The very nature of contemplation is difficult to grasp in his writings, which are more like contemplative meditations than doctrinal expositions. Evagrius found in Origen what was lacking in St. Gregory of Nazianzus, and he criticized St. Gregory of Nyssa in a circumspect way, without identifying him, for saying that union with God was an infinite progress in the darkness of ignorance superior to contemplation[18] For Evagrius the departure of the νοῦς (its ecstatic out-going) is not necessary, since by its very nature the νοῦς is the recipient of the divine light. Having once arrived at the state of purity, the νοῦς γυμνός, by beholding itself, beholds God who fills it with light. The receptivity of the νοῦς in the contemplation of the Trinity originates within its own nature: indeed it is perfectly νοῦς

[17]*Cent.* III, 8. Frankenberg, p. 257.
[18]*Cap. practica*, 59. PG. 40, col. 1236.

only to the extent that it is contemplating God. Here again
we find the fundamental idea of Origen, a basically Platonic
spiritualism, the kinship of the intelligible with the divine,
of the human νοῦς (as the image of God) with the Trinity.

The contemplation of the Holy Trinity is undifferentiated,
it has no degrees. Here again Evagrius' thought is not in
agreement with St. Gregory of Nyssa, for whom union with
God is an infinite progression of the soul. For Evagrius it
is a stable perfection which does not know the height or
depth, the "ascents" or "descents" which can occur in the
contemplation of created things.[19] The vision of the Holy
Trinity is always the same, just like the Trinity Himself
(ὄψις ἴση καθ' αὐτήν). Evagrius calls it "essential knowledge"—γνῶσις οὐσιώδης. This means that God is perceived immediately, without the intermediation of any image
whatever. There are no images of the divine ocean in the
νοῦς.[20] The divine light can be comprehended in no light
other than the radiance of the Holy Trinity. Actually, "in
the same way as the light which shows everything to us
needs no other light in order to be seen, so God who makes
us see everything needs no light in which we might see
him, since he is light by nature."[21]

Is this contemplation of the Trinity, or essential knowledge, the vision of the essence of God in Evagrius' doctrine?
It is difficult to make categorical pronouncements on this
point. On the one hand the object of vision for Evagrius is
always the light of the Trinity which shines in the pure
intellect; on the other hand, he never makes a distinction
between the nature of God and the essential light. However,
he does say "God is incomprehensible in himself,"[22] and
in Epis. 29: "Remember the true faith and know that the
Holy Trinity does not make himself known either to the
sight of corporeal beings or to the contemplation of incor-

[19]*Cent.* V, 63.
[20]*Letter to Menanius,* frag. 619.
[21]*Cent.* I, 35. Frankenberg, p. 79.
[22]*Cent.* II, 11. Frankenberg, p. 140.

poreal beings, unless he bows down through grace to the knowledge of the soul." ... "For creatures came into being out of nothing, while the knowledge of the Holy Trinity is essential and incomprehensible." This descent of the Holy Trinity through grace to the knowledge of the soul is, undoubtedly, the divine light which descends into the νοῦς during prayer.

Evagrius vigorously rejects all visible theophanies. He claims that this is a doctrine belonging to the wise men of the Gentiles (the Stoics) who imagined that God, having no form, assumes different appearances according to His will in order to appear to men.[23] "In aspiring to see the face of the Father who is in heaven, do not seek—at the time of prayer—to behold any form or figure after the manner of this world."[24] It is a demonic illusion which presents visions pleasing to the senses during prayer.[25]

An attempt has been made to see in these passages from Evagrius an allusion to the heterodox spirituality of the Euchites or Messalians which developed in the same period, in the fourth century. A synod in 383 condemned the doctrines of the Messalians, but this sect continued to exist for several centuries. Some of its tendencies will reappear, much later, among the Bogomils of Bulgaria and will be combatted ceaselessly by Byzantine Orthodoxy. Judging by certain Messalian propositions condemned in 383 and quoted by St. John Damascene and Timothy, priest of Constantinople, this sect professed a mystical materialism. The Messalians asserted that the essence of the Trinity could be perceived by the senses, by carnal eyes, that the Trinity transformed Himself into a single person in order to enter into union with the souls of the perfect, that God has taken different forms in order to reveal Himself to the senses, that only sensible revelations of God confer perfection upon

[23]*Letter* 29, Frankenberg, p. 587.
[24]*De Or.* 114. PG. 79, col. 1192.
[25]*Treatise on Prayer*, 72-3. Hausherr, p. 120f.

the Christian, that the state of freedom from passions is attained solely through prayer (hence the name of the Euchites—"Prayers"), that baptism and the sacraments are ineffective against the dominion of Satan over human nature, that those who have obtained proof of the state of impassibility by a sensible revelation of God, having been liberated from the Devil, can no longer be subjected to moral obligations or ecclesiastical discipline.

*   *   *

A study of the *Spiritual Homilies* attributed to St. Macarius, the founder of hermitages in the desert of Scete, has given Dom Vollecourt some reason to assert (in 1920) that this work, valued so much by Christian ascetics in all periods of history, is none other than the "Ascetikon" of the Messalians, condemned in 383. It cannot be denied that several of the Messalian propositions quoted by John Damascene and Timothy are found in the "Spiritual Homilies" ascribed to St. Macarius. However, the "Spiritual Homilies" cannot be criticized for heterodox excesses, e.g. the visibility of the essence of God, the grossly sensual character of grace, contempt for the sacraments, amoralism, etc. We may suppose that the Euchites represented the extreme wing of the mysticism of affection [trans: sentiment] found in the homilies attributed to St. Macarius, and that having belonged at first to the same spirituality they became separated later on. Fr. Stiglmayer, who cannot be accused of naïve credulity or the lack of critical spirit (indeed he often goes too far), refuses to regard the "Spiritual Homilies" as a Messalian text. He insists: (1) on the incompatibility of the content of the "Homilies" with Messalian doctrine; (2) on fact that *loca parallela* are not sufficient proof of identity; (3) that in spite of some traditions shared with the Messalians, the "Homilies" are orthodox as far as their doctrinal significance is concerned; and (4) that the disparate

elements in the "Homilies," originating in different periods, scarcely permit us to identify it with the ascetical book of the Messalians condemned in 383.

The spirituality of St. Macarius, or rather of the "Homilies" which bear his name, is the opposite of the intellectualistic mysticism of Evagrius. For St. Macarius (or pseudo-Macarius) the main difference between the Greek and Christian philosophers consists in the fact that the pagan sages drew their knowledge from reasoning, while the servants of God have divine knowledge. "We have tasted of God, we have had experience of him" (ἐγεύσαμεν καὶ πεῖραν ἔσχυμεν). Those who have experienced God can speak of Him. The moment of this experience (πεῖρα) is central to this spirituality and here, contrary to the mysticism of Evagrius, the experience has an affective character: it is addressed less to the intellect than to the senses. It is a mysticism of the consciousness of grace, of divine sensibility. Gnosis takes on here the meaning of consciousness, without which the way of union with God would be blind, "an illusory ascent" (ἄσκησις φαινομένη).[26]

Just as the Lord was clothed in a human body, so Christians must be clothed in the Holy Spirit. The Holy Spirit becomes the repose (ἡσυχία) of souls that are worthy, becomes their joy, their delight, their eternal life. God becomes food and drink, the "sweetness" (γλυκύτης) of the grace that we taste within. However, "he who enjoys illumination (φωτισμός) is greater and receives more than he who only tastes, for he has within himself the assurance of his visions (τίνα πληροφορίαν ὁράσεων). But there is something still greater: revelation (ἀποκάλυψις), in which the great mysteries of divinity are revealed to the soul. Those who reach this point see the image of the soul as we see the sun, but few have had this experience."[27]

An analogy can be seen here to Evagrius, all the more

26*Hom.* 40, 1. PG. 34, col. 761.
27*Hom.* 7, 5-6; ibid., col. 527.

so in that Macarius also refers to the substantial light of
the divinity in the soul (ὑποστατικοῦ φωτὸς ... ἔκλαμψις).[28] And yet this experience of grace is very different
from the intellectual contemplation of the divine light in
Evagrius, for whom it is a uniform and stable state under-
going no change. The "Spiritual Homilies" speak of the
fire of grace kindled by the Holy Spirit in the hearts of men,
making them burn like candles before the Son of God. This
divine fire follows the fluctuations in the human will; now
it is shining brilliantly as it embraces the entire being; now
it diminishes and no longer sheds its radiance in hearts that
are darkened by passions. "The immaterial and divine fire
illuminates the soul and puts it to the test. This fire descended
on the apostles in the form of tongues of flame. This fire
shone before Paul, it spoke to him, it illuminated his mind
and at the same time blinded his eyes, for the flesh cannot
endure the brightness of this light. Moses saw this fire in
the burning bush. This same fire lifted Elijah from the
ground in the form of a flaming chariot. . . . Angels and spirits
in the service of God participate in the brightness of this
fire. . . . This is the fire which pursues demons and exter-
minates sins. It is the power of resurrection, the reality of
eternal life, the illumination of holy souls, the stability of
celestial powers."[29]

   The Trinity dwells in the soul not as He is in Himself—
since no creature can receive Him in this way—but according
to man's capacity to receive Him.[30] The soul becomes the
"throne of God," it becomes altogether light, altogether a
face, altogether an eye; each of its members filled with
light, no place is left for darkness, as if it were full of
spiritual eyes (ὅλη ὀφθαλμῶν γέμουσα); on all sides it
is a "face" turned toward God, receiving the light of Christ
which enters within.[31] But in this world the kingdom of

[28]De Lib. ment. 22. PG. 34, col. 956.
[29]Hom. 5, 8. PG. 34, col. 513B.
[30]De Car. 28. PG. 34, col. 932.
[31]Hom. 1, 2. PG. 34, cols. 449-52.

light enlightens the soul secretly. It will be revealed in bodies glorified by light after the resurrection.[32] The eschatological moment is strongly emphasized in the *Spiritual Homilies:* the heavenly blessings (τὰ αἰώνια ἀγαθά) are reserved for those who love the Lord whom the Christians contemplate in the Holy Spirit, having their thoughts directed always toward heaven.[33] In these heavenly blessings God conforms Himself to creatures, becoming Jerusalem—the city of light, and Sion—the heavenly mountain, for the enjoyment and delight of His created beings.[34]

But above all the eyes of the soul must be fixed on Christ, who, like a good painter (καλὸς ζωγράφος), paints in those who believe in Him and constantly behold Him a portrait of the heavenly man, in His own image, by means of the Holy Spirit, out of the very substance of His ineffable light (ἐκ τοῦ αὐτοῦ Πνεύματος, ἐκ τῆς ὑπο-στάσεως αὐτοῦ τοῦ φωτὸς ἀνεκλαλήτου, γράφει εἰκόνα οὐράνιον).[35] The image is formed again in us according to the likeness, is clothed once more in the light of Holy Spirit, as Adam was before the fall.[36] Christ is both painter and model at the same time, and this is why in contemplating Him we are transformed into His likeness. The mystical language of the "Homilies" is far from being dogmatically precise. Thus we read in Homily 34 that in the age to come "all are transformed (μεταβάλλονται) into the divine nature." It is true that this expression is immediately qualified, i.e. "all repose in a single light," and there is elsewhere[37] the categorical assertion of the radical difference between the divine nature and created beings even in the state of union.

At the end of time ("the destruction of the firmament")

[32]*Hom.* 2, 5, cols. 465-8.
[33]*Hom.* 5, 4, col. 497.
[34]*Hom.* 4, 12, col. 481.
[35]*Hom.* 34, 1, col. 724.
[36]*Hom.* 12, 6 and 7, cols. 560-1.
[37]*Hom.* 49, 4, col. 816.

the righteous will live in the Kingdom, in light and glory,
seeing nothing other than Christ eternally in glory at the
right hand of the Father (μηδὲν ἕτερον ὁρῶντες, ἢ
καθὼς ὁ Χριστὸς ἐν δόξῃ ἐστὶ πάντοτε ἐν δεξιᾷ τοῦ
Πατρός).[38] Participants in the divine glory will be full
of consideration for one another and in this will shine all
the more brightly, progressing in the true vision of the
unspeakable light.[39] Thus the mysticism of affection, of
grace experienced here in this world, sensed as sweetness,
joy, or as an interior light of the soul, is fulfilled in the age
to come in communion with Christ in the light of His divinity.
The face to face vision, in which the soul becomes one whole
"spiritual eye," is a vision of Christ glorified.

*   *   *

Between the intellectualistic mysticism of Evagrius and
St. Macarius' mysticism of a life conscious of the experience
of grace a mid position is taken by Diadochus, Bishop of
Photice in Epirus. All that is known of him is that he was
one of the adversaries of the Monophysites, about the middle
of the fifth century. The critical edition of his works was
prepared in Russia by Popov in 1903 (in Kiev) and com-
pleted by Benedictov in 1908 (in St. Petersburg). A French
translation has appeared in the collection "Sources chrétiennes."

The goal for the Christian is union with God in love.
"Love," says Diadochus, "actually unites the soul to the
powers of God as it seeks by the inward sense the One
who is invisible."[40] This first maxim of the hundred chapters
on perfection contains implicitly the whole spiritual doctrine
of Diadochus of Photice: the invisible God with His δυνάμεις which will also be called energies, the union which

[38]*Hom.* 17, 4, col. 625.
[39]*Hom.* 34, 2, col. 745.
[40]*Cent.* I. Diadochus of Photice, *Spiritual Works.* Sources chrétiennes 5ᵃ,
p. 85.

is accomplished by ἀγάπη, and the organ of ἀγάπη seeking experience of the Divine, the inward sense which St. Diadochus also calls αἴσθησις νοηρά, αἴσθησις καρδίας, αἴσθησις πνεύματος, αἴσθησις τῆς ψυχῆς, πεῖρα αἰσθήσεως. Moved by love, we possess by the affection of the heart the One whom we honor by faith, and at the moment of this experience we are at a deeper level than faith.[41] As in the "Spiritual Homilies," the Holy Spirit first makes the soul taste the sweetness of God, but no one in this world can acquire a perfect experience of the Divine, "unless what is mortal has been entirely engulfed by life."[42] The one is the initial joy, the other is the consummation; the first is not free from vanity, the other has the strength of humility; between the two there is a blessed sadness and tears without sorrow.[43] In order to come to perfection the experience of God must be purified; this is why God abandons the soul and this instructive abandonment teaches it to seek God once more in humility.[44]

It is the divine light which perfects the human spirit, conferring likeness upon it through love. From the moment of baptism grace begins to paint the divine likeness over the image, like a portrait of God. "The inner sense reveals indeed that we are in the course of being formed in his likeness; but the perfection of this likeness we shall know only by illumination."[45] Here Diadochus follows Macarius very closely. But this theoretician of the mysticism of affection is more closely related to Evagrius when he firmly opposes the sensual mysticism of the Messalians: "It cannot be disputed that when the intellect begins to come frequently under the influence of the divine light it becomes completely transparent, to the point that it sees, itself, the riches of that light. It has been said that this happens when the power of

[41]*Cent.* 91, p. 153.
[42]*Cent.* 90, p. 152.
[43]*Cent.* 60, p. 120.
[44]*Cent.* 94, p. 155.
[45]*Cent.* 89, p. 149.

the soul gains control over the passions. But all that appears
to the soul as form, be it as light or as fire, comes from the
wiles of the Enemy; the divine Paul teaches this to us clearly
when he says that the Enemy disguises himself as an angel
of light."[46] "Let no one who hears about the affection of
the intellect hope that the glory of God will appear to him
visibly."[47] If the prophets saw God in a physical vision, "it
is not that he appeared to them changed into a visible figure,
but rather that they were among those who saw the Formless
One as in the form of glory, when his will and not his
nature was displayed to their eyes. For it was the active
Will which appeared physically in the vision of glory, God
having consented to let himself be seen entirely in the form
of his will."[48]

In the age to come God will be seen neither in His
nature nor in a figure but in the power of His glory. "This
is why those who are judged worthy will be constantly in
the light, always enjoying, in his glory, the love of God, but
they will be incapable of conceiving the nature of the light
of God which illuminates them; just as God in fact limits
himself when he wills to do so and yet remains unlimited, so
also he makes himself seen when he wills to do so and yet
remains invisible.

"And what must be understood as the power of God?

"A beauty without form which can be known only in
glory."[49]

The beauty or power of the divine nature (what Byzantine theologians will later designate, in dogmatic language,
by the term energies—ἐνέργειαι) is free of form because
it is the glory of the divine essence. However, this beauty
of the divine nature, its eternal light, will appear visible in
the age to come, ". . . because the Father, who has no form,
will show himself to us in the form and glory of the Son;

[46]*Cent.* 40, p. 108.
[47]*Cent.* 36, p. 105.
[48]*Vision* 12, p. 172.
[49]ibid., 14-15, p. 173.

it is for this reason in fact that it has pleased God that his Word should come to us by the Incarnation in human form and yet remain steadfast in the glory of His all-powerfulness, so that in beholding the concreteness of the figure of this glorious flesh (since form sees form) man might be able, having been purified, to see the beauty of the Resurrection as it applies to God."[50] We encountered the same concept in St. Irenaeus: the Father making the light of His nature shine in the Incarnate Son. This is the vision of God not in His nature, but in His glory (the beauty of His nature), the face to face vision of the person of Christ, of the Incarnate Son transfigured by the divine light.

Diadochus often speaks of gnosis, which he distinguishes from theology. Theology or wisdom (σοφία) is for him only the gift of teaching, while gnosis denotes the experience of union with God, an experience gained in prayer, in the perpetual recollection of God, in the uninterrupted invocation of the name of Jesus which instills it, "through intellectual recollection, in the ardour of the heart."[51] Thus the mysticism of the intellect and the mysticism of the heart are united, opening the way for a spirituality which will engage the whole nature of man. St. Diadochus of Photice may be regarded as one of the founders or at least as one of the precursors of Byzantine Hesychasm.

The sixth century will not be propitious for contemplative spirituality: the anti-Origen reaction, with the condemnation of Evagrius, will discredit mysticism in general, and a spirituality centered on the motion of the will or rather on the abnegation of the will—the cenobitic spirituality of St. Basil—will take precedence, together with the teaching of St. Barsanuphius and his disciple St. Dorotheus. But in the seventh century St. Maximus the Confessor will try to make a new synthesis and will bring all his breadth of understanding into the spiritual life—selecting certain valuable elements

[50]ibid., 21, p. 175.
[51]*Cent.* 59, p. 119.

from the thought of Evagrius—from the tradition of Origen—
in order to insert them into his work, nourished as it was on
a totally different tradition, the tradition of Dionysius
the Areopagite.

CHAPTER SEVEN

Saint Dionysius the Areopagite and Saint Maximus the Confessor

Byzantine theology on the vision of God will be more indebted to the work of a mysterious author known under the name of St. Dionysius the Areopagite than to Antioch and Alexandria. We do not have to occupy ourselves here with the origins of the Areopagite writings. All that we know about this collection of four treatises and ten epistles is the date when they were quoted for the first time. The Monophysites of Syria together with Severus of Antioch were the first to try, at the beginning of the sixth century, to cite the authority of St. Dionysius the Areopagite the disciple of St. Paul. But Orthodox writers will soon tear this weapon from their hands, commenting on the works of Dionysius and adapting them to the defence of their own cause. John of Scythopolis, in the sixth century, and especially St. Maximus in the seventh, will present the Areopagite corpus as evidence from within the Christian tradition. Despite some doubts about attributing the *Corpus* to Dionysius the disciple of St. Paul (St. Photius, for example, will remain sceptical on this point), the orthodoxy of the Areopagitic writings will never be questioned.

In 1900 Hugo Koch established the close connection of the *Corpus* of Dionysius with neo-Platonic thought, notably with Proclus, the last great Platonist of Alexandria (d. 486).

This connection had already been noted by St. Maximus, who claimed that Proclus had copied Dionysius. For Koch there is no doubt that the thought of the author of the *Corpus* depends on the last great pagan philosopher of Alexandria.

Common opinion would see in Dionysius (or pseudo-Dionysius) a Platonist with a tinge of Christianity, and his work as a channel through which neo-Platonist thought will be introduced again into the Christian tradition after Clement and Origen. After studying St. Dionysius it seems to me that just the opposite is true: here is a Christian thinker disguised as a neo-Platonist, a theologian very much aware of his task, which was to conquer the ground held by neo-Platonism by becoming a master of its philosophical method. Fr. Ceslas Péra is right when he says: "The position of Dionysius with regard to the thinkers of Greece is a relationship not of genetic dependency but of victorious opposition. He does not speak idly and there is no reason to doubt his sincerity when he mentions having been accused as a parricide for making impious use of the Hellenes against the Hellenes."[1] In this sense Dionysius stands in the tradition of the great Cappadocians, of St. Basil and especially St. Gregory of Nyssa, who dealt with similar themes.

What connects Dionysius to Gregory of Nyssa more than to the Alexandrian form of thought is the notion of divine darkness, as Puech has demonstrated very clearly in an article in *Etudes carmélitaines*.[2] Knowledge of God can only be attained by going beyond every visible and intelligible object. It is by ignorance (ἀγνωσία) that we know the One who is above all that can be an object of knowledge. It is not divine gnosis which is the supreme end, but the union (ἕνωσις) that surpasses all knowledge. As with St. Gregory of Nyssa, so also with Dionysius θεωρία is not the summit

---

[1] Ceslas Péra, "Denys le Mystique et la Theomachia," in *Revue des Sciences philosophiques et théologiques,* 1936, p. 62.

[2] H. Ch. Puech, "La ténèbre mystique chez le Pseudo-Denys l'Aréopagite et dans la tradition patristique," in *Etudes carmélitaines,* 1938, pp. 33-53.

of the ascent toward God. We grasp the unknowable nature of God in ignorance, by detaching ourselves from all His manifestations or theophanies.

Attempts have been made to connect this union with God through ignorance to the ecstasy of Plotinus. But here, as elsewhere in Dionysius' work, the kinship of expressions and a certain parallelism of themes suggest rather the intention of a Christian author who is trying to correct Plotinus. Human beings united to God are not simply identified with Him, they are "entirely in God" (ὅλους Θεοῦ γιγνομένους).[3] In the state of union we know God at a higher level than intelligence—νοῦς—for the simple reason that we do not know Him at all.[4] We have here the entry into darkness (σκότος), an entry concealed by the abundant light through which God makes Himself known in His beings. Knowledge is limited to what exists; now, as the cause of all being, God does not exist,[5] or rather He is superior to all oppositions between being and non-being. As with Plotinus, we must, according to Dionysius, leave the realm of beings in order to be united with God. However, the God of Dionysius is not the ἕν, the prime unity or identity of Plotinus, opposed to the multiplicity of beings. God is not unity, but the cause of unity, just as He is the cause of multiplicity. This is why Dionysius exalts the name of the Trinity, "the most sublime name,"[6] above the name "One." Again this is a point where Dionysius radically modifies the concept of Plotinus.

Unity and diversity, union and distinction appear even within God, in so far as He is Trinity—there are "unities and distinctions within the ineffable Unity and Substance,"[7] for the three persons are at the same time both unities and distinctions. But God makes Himself known by distinctions

---

[3]*The Divine Names*, VII, 1. PG. 3, col. 868A.
[4]*Mystical Theology*, I, 3. PG. 3. col. 1001.
[5]*The Divine Names*, I, 1, col. 588.
[6]ibid., XIII, 3, col. 981A.
[7]ibid., II, 5, col. 641.

(διακρίσεις) outside His nature—outside the "secret res-
idence enveloped in darkness and ignorance"—by proceeding
out of Himself in processions (πρόοδοι) or powers (δυνάμεις) which are His manifestations (ἐκφάνσεις), in
which created beings participate. By calling Him God, Life,
Substance, we mean the deifying, vivifying, substantiating
powers by which God communicates Himself while still remaining incommunicable by nature, and makes Himself
known while still remaining unknowable in His essence. While
they are distinct from the divine substance (ὕπαρξις), these
powers or operations are not really separated from it, because
in God "unities prevail over distinctions."[8] The δυνάμεις
are always God Himself, although outside His substance or
"unity." For "he distinguishes himself while remaining
simple, and multiplies himself without abandoning his unity."[9]

Here we recognize the distinction between the unknowable
οὐσία and the revelatory energies, according to which the
divine names are formed—a distinction which we saw in its
first outline in St. Basil and St. Gregory of Nyssa. This
distinction forms the pivot of the whole of Dionysius' theology. If this doctrine—as developed especially in Chapter
II of The Divine Names—is neglected (which has happened
all too often), then the central nerve of Dionysius' thought
will never be grasped; it will inevitably be interpreted in a
neo-Platonic sense which is alien to Dionysius' thought or
rather exactly opposed it. The δυνάμεις (or energies) of
Dionysius are not diminishing emanations from the divine
nature, which go ou in decreasing measure from the unity
of this nature into the lowest degrees of created being.
Dionysius insists on the integrity of the divine processions in
each degree of participation; this is why he often refers to
them in the singular, as the super-essential ray of the divine
darkness. Divinity is manifested fully and is wholly present
in the δυνάμεις, but created beings participate in it in

[9]ibid., col. 649.

the proportion or analogy proper to each one, hence the hierarchical order of the universe, which develops in an order of decreasing participations, of decreasing analogies in created beings. Dionysius' hierarchy definitely does not limit the plenitude of union; at every step of this ladder the union with God is realized fully, but the plenitude is not uniform, it is personal. In the analogy of each created nature there is an encounter, a synergy of two wills: the liberty of the creature, and the divine predetermination (προορισμός), the idea (παράδειγμα) or will addressing itself to each being. There is a double movement which runs through this hierarchical universe: God is manifested by His δυνάμεις in all beings, "is multiplied without abandoning his unity," and creatures are raised toward deification, transcending the manifestations of God in creation (the hierarchical illuminations) in order to enter the darkness, to attain the union above νοῦς, beyond all knowledge, all sensible or intelligible manifestations of God.

For Dionysius the two ways of knowledge, positive or contemplative theology and negative or apophatic theology, correspond to this double current which runs through creation. They are founded on the mysterious distinction within God Himself, between the revelatory δυνάμεις and the οὐσία or inaccessible "super-essence" (ὑπερουσιότης) — between movement toward distinction and the impetus toward unity. But what is dynamism in created natures is stability in God, where movement is at the same time also repose (ἡσυχία) for in the Persons of the Holy Trinity both unities and distinctions are identical.[10]

Both theological paths are necessary for the knowledge of God. But the negative way is more perfect. In the symbolic knowledge of the affirmative way Dionysius prefers names formed from material objects, less likely to lead into error those who are being raised to the contemplation of God. It is not as easy to confuse God with rock or fire as

[10]ibid., II, 4, col. 641; II, 5, col. 644.

it is to slip into the identification of the unknowable nature
with intelligence, the good, or being. Even in connection with
the Incarnation of the Word the negative way still holds
true, for "in the humanity of Christ," says Dionysius, "the
Super-essential is manifested in human nature without ceasing to be hidden behind this manifestation, or, to put it in
a more heavenly way, within the manifestation itself."[11]

Even in the vision of God among the blessed the perfect theophany does not exclude the negative way of union in non-
knowledge. "When," says Dionysius, "we become incorruptible
and immortal, having attained the state of beatitude, having become likenesses of Christ (χριστοειδοῦς), we shall be ever
with the Lord, according to the word of Scripture, enjoying His
visible theophany in purest contemplation (τῆς μὲν ὁρατῆς
αὐτοῦ θεοφανείας ἐν πανάγνοις θεωρίαις ἀποπλη-
ρούμενοι), illuminated by his radiant beams, just as the
disciples were illuminated at the time of his divine Transfiguration; at the same time, through our impassible and
immaterial intellect, we shall participate in his intelligible
illumination (νοητῆς αὐτοῦ φωτοδοσίας) and also in
the union above intelligence, in the incomprehensible and
blessed brightness of those more than radiant beams of light,
in a state similar to that of the heavenly spirits. For, according to the word of Truth, as sons of the resurrection we
shall be likenesses of the angels and sons of God."[12]

This text contains a synthesis of all that we have encountered so far in the Fathers of the first five centuries on
the subject of the vision of God. No trace of Origen's
spiritualism is left. It is the whole man, not just the spirit
or intellect (νοῦς), who enters into communion with God.
As in the writings of John Chrysostom and the school of
Antioch, it is the vision of the Incarnate Son. But for
Dionysius the doctrine of the spiritual senses (which is
missing in the Antiochene writers) finds its whole meaning

[11]*Letter* III. PG. 3, col. 1069B.
[12]*The Divine Names*, I, 4, col. 592.

in the "visible theophany," the vision of the light of the transfigured Christ. At the same time the intellect (νοῦς) receives an intelligible illumination, man *knows* God in this light—and here Dionysius again joins St. Gregory of Nazianzus and St. Cyril of Alexandria. But the human being surpasses all knowledge and transcends the νοῦς in a union which is an impulsive movement towards the unknowable nature, toward the darkness of the divine ἡσυχία—and here again we find the infinite progression of St. Gregory of Nyssa. Thus Christ is seen face to face and at the same time God manifests Himself fully, He is known in His revelatory διάκρισις; and yet in this union He surpasses all vision, all knowledge, for His super-essential nature remains always inaccessible.

With Dionysius we enter the world of truly Byzantine theology. His doctrine of dynamic manifestation, implying a distinction between the unknowable essence and its natural processions or energies (as they will be called, the term employed by the Cappadocians being adopted in preference to the δυνάμεις of Dionysius)—this distinction made by Dionysius will serve as the dogmatic foundation for the doctrine of the vision of God in later theology, especially in the fourteenth century. In the same way his doctrine of the ideas of God, likened to the predeterminations of His will and in this sense distinguished from the actual nature of God which is inaccessible to all external relationship, will become the common patrimony of Byzantine theologians.

It is sometimes said that the Areopagitic writings exercised a greater influence on the West than on the East. This is only superficially true; in the doctrinal landscape of Latin scholasticism, so different from that of the Byzantine tradition, the influence of Dionysius is indeed more striking, it draws more attention to itself. But as great as it may have been, this influence was only partial. The dynamic doctrine which determines the course of Byzantine thought has never been understood or adopted in the West. Even Erigena,

imbued with Dionysius and Maximus, was unable to grasp
the distinction between God's modes of existence in His
essence and in His external processions; this is why, having
distinguished the ideas of God from His essence, he placed
these ideas in the created order. If in the East the tradition
of Dionysius marks a definite triumph over Platonic
Hellenism, in the West, on the contrary, the work of
Dionysius, poorly assimilated, will often become the vehicle
for neo-Platonic influences.

* * *

Dionysius' *Corpus* was introduced into the stream of theological thought as a witness to the Christian tradition by
St. Maximus the Confessor (580-662). The thought of St.
Maximus seeks to make a synthesis, to unite the disparate
elements of the treasury of theology around one central
idea, around that aspect of Christology which he developed
through the whole course of his life. This was the dogma
of the two wills and two natural energies united in Christ,
a dogma for which he gave his life. "The mystery of the
Incarnation of the Word," says St. Maximus, "contains the
meaning of all the symbols and enigmas of Scripture, as
well as the meaning concealed in the whole of sensible and
intelligible creation. He who knows the mystery of the
Cross and the Tomb knows also the essential causes of all
things. Finally, he who penetrates still further and is initiated
into the mystery of the Resurrection, learns the end for
which God created all things in the beginning."[13] Thus the
economy of the Incarnate Son reveals three successive levels
to us, one after another: it attains being (εἶναι) through
the Incarnation; it attains well being (εὖ εἶναι), conform-
ing to the ideas or prescriptions of the divine will for created
beings, through the incorruptibility of the will leading to
the Cross; it attains eternal being (ἀεὶ εἶναι), the incor-

[13]*Gnostic Cent.* I, 66. PG. 90, col. 1108AB.

ruptibility of nature which is revealed beyond the Cross and the Tomb, through the Resurrection.[14] The three stages of perfection established by Origen and developed by Evagrius of Pontus will be transformed and re-created out of this Christological scheme. The πρακτική corresponds to being, to the reality of the body of Christ; knowledge of the natures of beings, of their divine ideas or preconceptions, corresponds to well-being, to the soul of Christ, to His incorruptible will (which excludes the intellectualistic character of gnosis); finally, θεολογία which corresponds to eternal being, consists of two stages: "the simple mystagogy of theological science"—the degree corresponding to the human spirit of Christ, where there is room for the mysticism of Evagrius, the contemplation of the deified νοῦς filled with the light of the Trinity—and the superior degree, which is entered by surpassing or going out of the νοῦς toward the divinity of Christ, "by perfect negation toward perfect indetermination." This is the ecstatic way of Dionysius, the way of union in an ignorance which surpasses all knowledge.

St. Maximus has made use of Evagrius to a great extent, especially in his *Annals on Love*. Fr. Viller[15] has gone so far as to assert St. Maximus's close dependence on the thought of Evagrius: St. Maximus is simply a compiler who adjusted discordant elements as best he could, juxtaposing the apophaticism of Dionysius and Evagrius' contemplation of the divine light in the νοῦς. This has always seemed to us an injustice. Today, after Fr. von Balthazar's study on the thought of St. Maximus, no one can doubt the originality of this powerful synthesis.

"The spirit is perfect," says Maximus, "when by the grace of true faith it possesses in super-ignorance the super-knowledge of the super-incomprehensible" (τὸν ὑπεράγνω- στον ὑπεραγνώστως ὑπεραγνωκὼς)—this is from

[14]*Ambigua*. PG. 91, col. 1392.
[15]"Aux sources de la spiritualité de s. Maxime: les oeuvres d'Evagre le Pontique." RAM, 1930, pp. 153-84, 239-68, 331-6.

Dionysius; what follows refers to the knowledge of God
in beings, to θεωρία: "[The spirit is perfect] when it comprehends the universal causes in creatures (for Maximus and
Dionysius, the ideas or wills of God); when by the action
within them of divine Providence and Judgment it has received from God the knowledge which comprehends all
things. All, of course, that it is possible for man to comprehend."[16] If this is from Evagrius, his thought is transformed on the basis of Dionysius' energetism. We pass from
"physical gnosis" of created beings to theology or divine
knowledge, obtaining the "grace of divine comprehension
(θεολογικὴ χάρις), surpassing the knowledge of creatures
"on the aisles of love" in order to "be in God." "Then, so
far as it is possible for the human spirit, we enter fully
into the nature of his divine attributes by the Holy Spirit."[17]
This is the degree of contemplation corresponding to the spirit
of Christ, the summit of knowledge possible for created
beings, where we perceive the attributes or energies (the
δυνάμεις of Dionysius) by which God makes Himself
known: He who is above is known in ignorance, by surpassing the νοῦς. "On the threshold of the knowledge of
God, do not seek to know his essence; a human spirit cannot
attain to such knowledge; no one knows it but God. But
consider fully (in so far as you are able) His attributes, for
example his eternity, his infinity, his invisibility, his goodness, his wisdom, his power which creates, governs and judges
all beings. For among all men that one merits the name
of theologian who seeks to discover, if only in part, the
truth of his attributes."[18] "God, and so also the divine, is
comprehensible from a certain point of view, incomprehensible from others. Comprehensible in the contemplation of
his attributes, incomprehensible in the contemplation of his
essence."[19] "We do not know God in his essence but by the

[16]*Cent. on Charity,* III, 999. Trans. Pégon, Sources chrétiennes 9, p. 151.
[17]ibid., II, 26, p. 101.
[18]ibid., II, 27, pp. 101-2.
[19]ibid., IV, 7, p. 153.

magnificence of his creation and the action of his Providence
which present to us, as in a mirror, the reflection of his
goodness, his wisdom and his infinite powers."[20] (His attributes or energies are known through created beings.)
"The purified mind either has simple and pure representations of human things, or naturally contemplates visible and
invisible beings, or receives the light of the Holy Trinity."[21]
(This is the supreme degree of θεωρία.) "But having come
to God, the ardour of his desire makes him seek first the
divine essence, for he finds no consolation in anything that
is a resemblance. But this is an impossible task and the
knowledge of the essence of God is inaccessible to all created
natures. He therefore contents himself with the attributes,
i.e. the eternity, infinity, invisibility, goodness, wisdom, and
the power which creates, governs and judges beings. One
thing only is perfectly comprehensible in God: that he is infinite; and the fact of knowing nothing is already a knowledge transcending the spirit, as the theologians Gregory and
Dionysius have shown."[22]

The distinction between the nature and attributes or
between the unknowable essence and the revelatory powers
or energies of God is expressly affirmed, following Dionysius
and the Cappadocians. In the plan for communion with God
the contemplation of God in beings or in the mirror of the
soul is opposed to the union with God in ignorance which
surpasses all knowledge. Indeed we know that in which we
participate; but since the essence is incapable of being participated in by definition (we are not and can never be God
by essence), we must leave the realm of participation and
renounce all knowledge in being united with God. If from
knowledge of creatures we are raised to the knowledge of
God's attributes, it is because beings participate in His
revelatory powers, his energies. "Rational and spiritual nature

[20] ibid., I, 96, p. 91.
[21] ibid., I, 97, p. 91.
[22] ibid., I, 100, pp. 91-2.

partakes of the holy God by its very nature, by its ability
to be good (I mean by its capacity for goodness and wisdom),
and by the free gift of eternal life. It is by this participation that it knows God."[23] Life and eternal life are stable
participations accorded to the very essence of rational
creatures. The εὖ εἶναι (well being, i.e. goodness and
wisdom) is accorded to their free will in order that "what
God is in his essence his creature may become by participation." We have here the image (participation accorded to
essences) and the likeness (participation accorded to wills),
creation and deification. "It is not at all out of some need
that God, the absolute plenitude, has brought his creatures
into being, it is so that these creatures might be blessed in
taking part in his likeness, and that he might rejoice in the
joy of his creatures, while they inexhaustibly draw from the
Inexhaustible."[24]

Deification is the central idea of the spirituality of St.
Maximus. With Evagrius it accompanies contemplation, or
rather it is revealed in its superior stages of pure prayer
as the natural state of the voῦς, the recipient of the divine
light. For St. Maximus deification, the supreme end of the
human will, determines all the rest. Instead of being simply
added to Evagrius' system, as Fr. Viller claims, the ecstacy
of Dionysius, the surpassing of being (the union in ignorance) transforms this system from top to bottom. It
communicates to the whole way of ascent to God the dynamism which we have noticed in Dionysius, the impulse
to go beyond, to depart out of limited nature in the quest
for union with God. It is no longer gnosis, as in Evagrius,
but rather ἀγάπη which is primary in the doctrine of St.
Maximus. Fr. Pegon, translator of the *Annals of Love*, has
drawn attention to this. "The knowledge of God," he says,
"is not the goal of charity in the sense that would make
charity purely a means to an end. We would speak more

[23]ibid., III, 24, p. 130.
[24]ibid., III, 46, p. 137.

accurately if we said that knowledge is the *effect,* the *sign* of the union with God brought about by love, but an effect which reacts in turn on the cause, intensifying love."[25] Maximus is closer here to St. Gregory of Nyssa and Dionysius than to Evagrius.

"In order to love God, who transcends all reason and knowledge, who is free from all relationship (σχέσεως) and nature (φύσεως), we must in an irresistible leap surpass the sensible and intelligible, time and the aeon and space (τόπος), we must be totally deprived of all energy of the senses, thought and νοῦς, in order to encounter inexpressibly and in ignorance (ἀρρήτως τε καὶ ἀγνώστως) the divine delights, above thought and intelligence."[26] Those who have followed Christ in action and contemplation will be changed into an ever better condition, and there is not time to tell of all the ascents and revelations of the saints who are being changed from glory to glory, until each one in order (ἐν τῷ ἰδίῳ τάγματι) receives deification.[27] In the final state of the age to come human beings are called to unite in themselves "created and uncreated nature by love, so that they appear in unity and identity by the acquisition of grace."[28] This union by grace which is accomplished in created persons is analogous, for St. Maximus, to the hypostatic union of the two natures in Christ. Maximus never loses sight of the Christology which is central to his thought. Now, if the transition from the mind of Christ to His divinity is accomplished for us by way of negation, of ecstatic ignorance, the divine nature penetrates His humanity by its energies no less than His mind penetrates His body and soul. This "perichoresis" or dynamic co-penetration of what is created and uncreated in Christ finds its analogy in beings who are striving to become "gods by grace." In fact they begin to be above matter (with reference

[25]op. cit., Introduction, p. 55.
[26]*Amb.,* PG. 91, col. 1153BC.
[27]ibid., col. 1364A.
[28]ibid., col. 1308B.

to the body) by action ... above form (with reference to
the mind) by contemplation. They attain to a stage above
the combination of form and matter which is the condition
of things in this world.[29] Therefore from the first stage on-
ward the way of Christian perfection (in πρᾶξις as well
as in θεωρία) is the way of deification enabling us to
transcend by grace the limitations of nature, which of course
totally alters the perspective of Evagrius. Deification involves
the whole human being. "While remaining in his soul and
body entirely man by nature, he becomes in his soul and
body entirely god in grace, by the divine splendor of the
beatifying glory which is wholly expedient to him" (ὅλος
μὲν ἄνθρωπος μένων κατὰ ψυχὴν καὶ σῶμα διὰ τὴν
φύσιν, καὶ ὅλος γινόμενος θεὸς κατὰ ψυχὴν καὶ
σῶμα διὰ τὴν χάριν καὶ τὴν ἐμπρέπουσαν αὐτῷ
διόλου θείαν τῆς μακαρίας δόξης λαμπρότητα).[30]

How does St. Maximus conceive the vision of God in
the deified state of the age to come? As we might expect
from what has been said, it cannot be the vision of the
divine essence. "Dionysius affirms," says St. Maximus, "that
no one has seen or will ever see the hidden reality (that
which is hidden in God: αὐτὸ μὲν τὸ κρύφιον τοῦ Θεοῦ),
i.e. his essence (ὅπερ οὐσία αὐτοῦ). Or, with still greater
sublimity, that no one can or will be able to overtake in
thought or express (κατανοῆσαι καὶ φράσαν) what God
is in himself" (τὶ ἐστὶν ὁ Θεός).[31] As with Dionysius, the
vision of the elect is presented as a dynamic revelation of
the divinity of Christ's Person, the God-Man: His divine
body will be a visible theophany (τὸ θεῖον αὐτοῦ σῶμα
ὁρατὴν θεοφάνειαν φύσιν) and at the same time the
elect participate by the spirit in the intelligible (νοητὴ)
theophany "in the most perfect way."[32] However, it would

[29]ibid., col. 1273C.
[30]ibid., col. 1088C.
[31]Scholiae on the Celestial Hierarchy IV, 3. PG. 4, col. 55.
[32]Scholiae on the Divine Names I, 4. PG. 4, col. 197.

seem that the sensible and intelligible will no longer be opposed to one another as two different orders of knowledge, since, says St. Maximus, being deified "we shall be uniformly one (ἐνοειδῶς ἕν), free from diversities due to mixture" (τῶν κατὰ σύνθεσιν ἑτεροτήτων ἡμῶν).[33] We have here a vision of God which surpasses the intellect as well as the senses; for this reason it is addressed to the whole man; a communion of personal man with the personal God.

With Dionysius and Maximus we enter Byzantine theology properly so called. This body of thought makes a distinction between God's unknowable οὐσία and His manifestations (dynamic attributes, δυνάμεις or energies), a distinction which, instead of limiting the mystical flight by placing the human being before a closed door, opens up an infinite path beyond knowledge.

[33]ibid.

CHAPTER EIGHT

Saint John Damascene
and Byzantine Spirituality

Before examining the development of the spirituality of
Dionysius and Maximus among the Byzantine contemplatives,
we must dwell for a moment on certain aspects of the
vision of God touched upon indirectly in dogmatic discussions.

I shall only point out a rather interesting passage in the
work of St. Anastasius the Sinaite, abbot of the monastery
on Mount Sinai, the "new Moses" as he was called, who
died at the beginning of the eighth century. In his polemical
work against the Monophysites, entiled Ὁδηγὸς (The
Guide),[1] St. Anastasius accuses his adversaries of confusing the nature (φύσις) and the πρόσωπον in God, the
second term being used usually to signify person, although
it means literally "face." In order to support his distinction
between the φύσις and the πρόσωπον, St. Anastasius
refers to the Gospel text on the angels of little children who
always behold the face (πρόσωπον) of their heavenly
Father. The impossibility of seeing the nature (φύσις) of
God seems so evident that St. Anastasius is content simply
to quote this text in order to prove that the πρόσωπον
is something different from the φύσις. He refers then to
the passage in the First Epistle to the Corinthians on the
face to face vision of God, pointing out that it says πρόσω-

[1]Ch. 8. PG. 89, col. 132.

137

πον πρὸς πρόσωπον and not φύσις πρὸς φύσιν. It is
not nature which sees nature, but person who sees person.
The same idea is expressed by the defenders of icons in
the epoch of controversy with the iconoclasts. The iconoclastic
synod of 754 appealed against the cult of icons to the following argument, formulated by the Emperor Constantine V:
What do the icons represent of Christ? If we say that they
are the two natures combined, we fall into Monophysitism by
confusing His divinity and His humanity, and we compound
the error by wishing to circumscribe the divinity within an
image. If on the contrary we say that the icon represents
only the humanity of Christ, we plunge into Nestorianism,
separating the two inseparable natures. St. Theodore the
Studite gave the Orthodox reply to this iconoclastic argument by formulating the nature of the dissimilarity and the
similarity between the image and its prototype. The image
is always dissimilar to the prototype with regard to essence
(κατ' οὐσίαν), but it is similar to it with regard to hypostasis (καθ' ὑπόστασιν) and name (κατ' ὄνομα). It is
the hypostasis of the Incarnate Word, and not His divine
or human nature which is represented in the icons of Christ.[2]
This dogmatic basis for the cult of icons is very important
for the doctrine of the vision of God: it refers to a communion with the person of Christ in which the energies of
the two natures, created and uncreated, interpenetrate one
another. This last idea will be developed, after St. Maximus,
by St. John Damascene (d. 749).

* * *

St. John Damascene begins his exposition of *The Orthodox
Faith* with a categorical affirmation of the unknowable nature
of God. "Neither men, nor the celestial powers, nor the
cherubim and the seraphim can know God other than in
his revelations. By nature he is above being and therefore

[2] *Antirrhetic,* III. PG. 99, col. 405B.

above knowledge. We can only designate his nature apophatically, by negations. What we say of God affirmatively (κατσφατικῶς) does not indicate his nature, but his attributes—that which is near to his nature" (τὰ περὶ τὴν φύσιν).[3] These are the manifestations *ad extra*, the δυνάμεις of Dionysius, the energies of the Cappadocians. Damascene speaks of the energies particularly in the context of Christology, distinguishing, with St. Maximus, the divine and human energies within the God-Man. What ought to interest us particularly is his application of the doctrine of energies to the Transfiguration, the manifestation of divinity in the Incarnate Word. St. John Damascene deals twice with this subject, in his *Exposition of the Orthodox Faith*,[4] and in a homily on the Transfiguration.[5] "The body (of Christ) was glorified at the same time that it was brought out of nonbeing into existence, that the glory of the divinity should be spoken of also as the glory of the body" (καὶ ἡ τῆς θεότητος δόξα καὶ δόξα τοῦ σώματος λέγεται). ". . . never was this holy body alien to the divine glory."[6] In the Transfiguration Christ did not become what he was not before, but appeared to his disciples as he was, by opening their eyes, by giving sight to those who were blind.[6a] It was the same person of the Incarnate Word which the disciples beheld on Mount Tabor, but they had received the faculty of contemplating the person of Christ in its eternal glory, of perceiving the energy of the divne nature. "For everything becomes one in God the Incarnate Word: what pertains to the flesh as well as what is of the infinite divinity (τῆς ἀπεριγράπτου θεότητος). However, we see that the glory that was shared has a different source than the passibility that was shared. The divine triumphs (over the created) and communicates to the body the radiance belonging to its

---

[3]Ch. IV. PG. 94, col. 800.
[4]ibid. Ch. XVIII. PG. 94, col. 1188BC.
[5]PG. 96, cols. 564-5.
[6]ibid., col. 564.
[6a]ibid.

glory, while still remaining in itself (as divine nature) non-participant in the passions, in the passible."[7] Here we have the application of the doctrine of energies to Christology: the divine nature remains inaccessible in itself, but its nature, its eternal glory penetrates created nature and communicates itself to it. Within the hypostatic union the humanity of Christ participates in the divine glory, and enables us to see God.

St. John Damascene asks himself why St. Basil calls the Eucharist "image" (ἀντίτυπα) of the body and blood of Christ. He called it an image, he says in reply, in relation to the realities of the age to come. This does not mean that the Eucharist is not truly the body and blood of Christ, but that now we participate in divinity in the Eucharistic species, while then we shall participate in divinity with our whole consciousness, by vision only (διὰ μόνης τῆς θέας). By participation in the divine glory "the righteous and the angels will shine like the sun in eternal life, together with our Lord Jesus Christ, eternally seeing him and eternally being seen by him, drawing from him an unending joy, praising him with the Father and the Holy Spirit in the ages of ages."[8] The face to face vision is a communion with the person of Christ, a reciprocal relationship—we see and are seen—a vision-participation in divinity in the divine glory which makes the righteous shine like stars.

St. John Damascene, a Byzantine scholastic who recapitulated the doctrines of the Fathers of the Christological period, i.e. of the first seven centuries, determines the doctrine of the vision of God in the perspective of Christological dogma for the whole of subsequent theology in Byzantium. But there is another aspect of the doctrine of the vision of God which St. John did not develop: this is the subjective side, touching on the communion of the whole person of man with God, a question which is raised on the level of pneuma-

[7]ibid., col. 565.
[8]De fide orthodoxa, IV, 27. PG. 94, col. 1228.

tological dogma. We have seen, in the work of St. Cyril of Alexandria, a clear exposition of the role of the Holy Spirit in communion with God. It is in the Holy Spirit that we participate in the beauty (κάλλος) of the divine nature; it is in Him that the divinity of the Word appears to us, so that by contemplating the Incarnate Son "we no longer know him according to the flesh," but in the glory proper to His divinity. And yet the flesh is not extraneous to this experience, since it is the body of Christ which is transfigured by the divine light.

* * *

This pneumatological aspect of the vision of God is expressed especially in spirituality as the experience of grace. In examining the ascetical doctrines which refer to contemplation we have been able to distinguish two deviations: the intellectualism of Evagrius with its source in Origen and the latter's Platonic spiritualism, and the Messalians' sensual experience of God, where God is materialized and takes on sensible forms as He enters into communion with men. Between the two there is the mysticism of affection, of grace that is felt, experienced, the mysticism of the "Spiritual Homilies" attributed to St. Macarius, and the doctrine of contemplation of St. Diadochus of Photice, more sober than that of Macarius, suspicious of all sensible depiction, but alien to the intellectualism of Evagrius. With Dionysius and Maximus, as we have tried to show, Evagrius' intellectualism is radically surpassed in the ecstatic leap, in going beyond the limits of created nature toward the union with God who surpasses all knowledge, all gnosis, the gnosis of affection as well as that of intellectual contemplation. By action and contemplation man, "carried along the aisles of love," goes (according to St. Maximus) above and beyond the composition of form and matter. Being raised to the deified state he transcends the opposition between the sensible and the

intelligible which both belong to the realm of created being.
This is why the reality which appears to contemplation, not
being of the created order, cannot be adequately designated.
It is Isaac of Syria who says, in the middle of the seventh
century: "The realities of the age to come have no clear and
direct name. With regard to these things we can have only
a certain simple knowledge..." And he repeats the words
of Dionysius: "This is the ignorance which surpasses all
knowledge."[9] The thought of Dionysius, adopted by Maximus,
will serve as the doctrinal basis for mysticism in which the
whole man, in the totality of his being, will be involved in
communion with God. I do not mean that this spirituality did
not exist before St. Maximus, for already in Diadochus of
Photice in the fifth century we have noticed this union of
the heart and intellect (νοῦς) in prayer, which is the fundamental characteristic of spirituality known under the name
of Hesychasm.

The Hesychasts have never had a good press in the West.
The reason for this is in particular the bad faith of certain
modern critics who have wanted to mix confessional disputes
with the study of a question in the history of spirituality.
I shall try not to follow their example in making an apology
for Hesychasm, all the more so in that this question touches
the subject of our study only indirectly. But some altogether
erroneous opinions concerning what has been called
Hesychastic prayer must be dispelled:

First of all Hesychasm is not a spiritual movement but
simply a form of monastic life devoted entirely to prayer.

Next, this art of prayer, contrary to all that has been
said about the Hesychasts, is not a mechanical process
designed to induce ecstacy; far from seeking mystical states,
the Hesychastic monks tend toward νῆψις, sobriety, to interior attentiveness, the union of the intellect and heart and
the control of the heart by the intellect, the "watching of
the heart" by the mind, the "silence of the heart" (ἡσυχία);

[9]Ed. Wensink, II, pp. 8-9.

this is the appropriate Christian expression of ἀπάθεια, where action and contemplation are not conceived as two different orders of life, but on the contrary are merged in the exercise of "spiritual action"—πρᾶξις νοερά.

In the third place, spiritual action involves a technique of prayer tending to mastery over the body and soul, but this certainly does not mean that the Hesychastic method is nothing but an external procedure leading to the mechanization of prayer.

Fourth, the contemplation of the blessings of the age to come, of divine realities and of uncreated light, is not the goal of the Hesychast, but an expression of the communion with God which he is seeking constantly.

Finally, Hesychasm is not the fairly recent invention of Byzantine monks, for characteristic elements of what is called Hesychastic prayer are found in the writings of Diadochus, St. John Climacus, Hesychius of Sinai. The first systematic exposition of the technique of interior prayer known to us is attributed to St. Simeon the New Theologian. Even if it was actually written in a later period, it nonetheless reflects an ancient tradition.

＊　　＊　　＊

St. Simeon, who has been given the name "New Theologian" by the Byzantine tradition ("new" after St. Gregory of Nazianzus, called Gregory the Theologian), lived in the end of the tenth and in the first half of the eleventh centuries. His death occurred, in all probability, in 1022. It is very difficult (if not impossible at this time) to analyze the works of St. Simeon with a view to making a precise judgment on his doctrine of the vision of God. The edition of his works which appeared in Smyrna in 1886 is practically unavailable. Even Krumbacher has been unable to refer to it. A modern Greek translation prior to the publication of the original text was made by Dionysius Zagoraios and

published in Venice in 1790. This edition is also very rare
and the Russian translation of this new Greek text cannot
be considered as a reliable source. Migne has published a
Latin translation made by Pontanus in 1603—including 33
sermons and 40 hymns, to which he added two pamphlets
of Simeon's of lesser importance, in Greek. Finally some
original texts of St. Simeon are to be found in Holl and
Hausherr.[10] Let us try nevertheless to become acquainted
with the doctrine of the vision of God in the thought of
Simeon the New Theologian, if not in its precise formula-
tions, at least in its general characteristics.

St. Simeon developed the idea of ὁρατὴ θεοφανεία
which we have found in the work of Dionysius, Maximus
and Damascene. But while St. Maximus and St. John
Damascene speak of the vision of the divine glory especially
within the context of Christology, with reference to the
deified humanity of Christ through which we participate in
the ἔκλαμψις or divine illumination, St. Simeon considers
the same reality, only on the level of pneumatology. For
him it involves above all a revelation of the Holy Spirit
in us, the life in grace which cannot remain hidden but
manifests itself, on the higher plain of eternal life, as light.

Modern critics are so obsessed with the idea of Messalianism that they are ready to find it wherever the vision
of divine light is mentioned. However, the chief source
of our knowledge of Messalianism is precisely St. John
Damascene, who, in connection with the Transfiguration,
as we have seen, develops a doctrine of the vision of the
divine glory which some critics would certainly have accused
of Messalianism if they had found it in the work of a
"Hesychastic" author. But when they have a clear-cut prej-
udice they pass over troublesome texts in silence, instead

[10]"Sources chrétiennes" (No. 51) published *Chapitres théologiques,
gnostiques et pratiques* in 1957, and is preparing an edition of Simeon's
Catecheses (with critical text) under the supervision of Mgr. Basile
Krivochéine.

of using them to clarify what it is that Damascene objects to in the Messalian doctrine. And yet he has clearly said: What is heterodox is the Messalians' claim to have actually perceived the divine essence by means of the bodily senses.

Returning to St. Simeon, we can ask ourselves what is the nature of the vision of the divine light which constitutes the central theme of the bulk of his writings? Is it a sensible or an intellectual perception? St. Simeon does not tell us, and when he speaks of the experience of the divine and un-created light he uses contradictory expressions. He affirms its visibility, and at the same time calls it "invisible light":

"Εστι πῦρ τὸ θεῖον ὄντως
"Ακτιστον, ἀορατόν γε, ἄναρχον καὶ ἄϋλον τε
ἀπερίγραπτον ὡσαύτως,
'Αναλλοίωτον εἰσάπαν,
"Ασβεστον, ἀθάνατον, ἀπερίληπτον πάντῃ
"Εξω πάντων τῶν κτισμάτων.[11]

"It is a truly divine fire, uncreated and invisible, eternal and immaterial, perfectly steadfast and infinite, inextin-guishable and immortal, incomprehensible, beyond all cre-ated being." This light "has separated me from all being visible and invisible, granting me a vision of the uncreated One. . . . I am united with the One who is uncreated, incor-ruptible, infinitely invisible to all."[12]

As with Dionysius this is a departure out of created being, a union in ignorance. This is why—as with Dionysius and Maximus—the eternal realities in which we participate are strictly speaking neither sensible nor intelligible; but precisely because they transcend the intellect as well as the senses they are perceived by the whole man and not by just one of his faculties. "God is light," says St. Simeon, "and he communicates his brightness to those who are

[11]Ed. Smyrna, 1886, II, 1, 1.
[12]ibid.

united with him, to the extent that they are purified. Then
the extinguished light of the soul, i.e. the darkened spirit,
knows that it is rekindled, because the divine fire has em-
braced it. O miracle! Man is united to God spiritually and
corporeally, for his soul is in no way separated from the
spirit, nor the body from the soul. God enters into union
with the whole man.''[13] We are very far here from the intellectualistic mysticism of Origen and Evagrius, from the
escape out of the sensible toward the intelligible. But we
are just as far also from the sensible perceptions of the
Messalians. The Alexandrians spiritualized the sensible, the
Messalians materialized the spiritual. Here the divine light
is presented to the whole man, to the whole person, as an
uncreated reality transcending both spirit and matter. If we
wish to see this as a spiritual flight, this is not a flight from
the sensible but a radical departure out of the realm of
created being toward the deifying union with God. If on
the contrary we wish to see this experience as a materialization of the divine, it will be necessary to speak rather of
a transfiguration of created nature, of body and soul, by
the divine grace which appears as the uncreated light in
which man as a whole participates. At any rate light signifies
for Simeon an encounter with God: whether it be man who
is raised toward God or God who descends toward man.

"I have often seen the light," says St. Simeon, "sometimes it has appeared to me within myself, when my soul
possessed peace and silence, sometimes it has appeared only
at a distance, and at times it was even hidden completely.
Then I experienced great affliction, believing that I would
never see it again. But from the moment when I began to
shed tears, when I bore witness to a complete detachment
from everything, and to an absolute humility and obedience,
the Light appeared once again, like the sun which dissipates
the thickness of the clouds and reveals itself little by little,
bringing joy. Therefore thou, Unspeakable, Invisible, Un-

[13]*Sermon* 25. Ed. of Mount Athos (Russian) I, p. 228.

touchable One, moving all things, revealing thyself and hiding thyself at every hour, thou hast disappeared and appeared before me day and night. Slowly thou hast dispelled the darkness which was in me, thou hast dissipated the cloud which covered me, thou hast opened my spiritual hearing, thou hast purified the pupil of the eye of my spirit. Finally having formed me according to thy will, thou hast revealed thyself to my shining soul, becoming invisible to me once more. And suddenly thou didst appear as another sun, O ineffable divine condescension."[14] "I give thanks to thee for this that thou, the divine Being above all beings, hast deigned to make thyself one spirit with me, without confusion, without alteration. . . . I give thee thanks for having revealed thyself to me as the day without end, as the sun that never sets, O thou, who hast no place to hide thyself; for thou hast never hidden thyself from sight, never hast thou despised any one, but rather it is we who have hidden ourselves, unwilling to approach Thee."[15]

In the experience of the divine light in St. Simeon's writings there is no trace of the depersonalizing ecstatic state, where human consciousness is lost in the contemplation of an impersonal divinity. On the contrary it is precisely the communion with a personal God which renders the experience of His light inexpressible in human language. What St. Simeon attempts to express here in contradictory terms gives us a glimpse of this communion with God dwelling in His uncreated light: "When we attain perfection," he says, "God no longer comes to us as before without appearance and without image. . . . He comes under a certain image, and yet it is the image of God. For God does not appear in any figure or sign whatever, but makes himself seen in his simplicity, formed out of formless, incomprehensible, ineffable light. I can say no more. Nevertheless he

[14]*Sermon* 90; ibid., II, pp. 487-9. Fr. trans. in *Vie Spirituelle* No. 28 (1931), pp. 76-7.
[15]*Introduction to Hymns on the Divine Love.* PG. 120, col. 509.

makes himself seen clearly, he is perfectly recognizable, he speaks and hears in a way that cannot be expressed. He who is God by nature converses with those whom he has made gods by grace, as a friend converses with his friends, face to face. He loves his sons as a Father; he is loved by them beyond all measure. He becomes in them a wondrous knowledge, a dreadful hearing. They cannot speak of him as they ought, nor can they any longer keep silence. . . . The Holy Spirit becomes in them all that the Scriptures say about the Kingdom of God, the pearl, the grain of mustard seed, the leaven, water, fire, bread, beverage of life, marriage, the marriage chamber, the bridegroom, friend, brother and father. But what can I say about the Unspeakable One? He whom the eye has not seen, nor the ear heard. He who has not yet come into the heart of man, how can he be expressed in words? Although we may have received and acquired all this within ourselves, as a gift of God, we can in no way measure it by the intellect or express it in words."[16]

These are the realities of the age to come which can be glimpsed here below—in ecstacy at first, but in a constant communion with the divine in those who are more nearly perfect. For ecstasies and ravishings are only suitable, according to St. Simeon, to the inexperienced, to those whose nature is not yet adapted to the experience of the Uncreated One.[17] However, this new reality is present in all Christians, for it is nothing other than baptismal grace. St. Simeon often repeats this. The sacramental element is strongly emphasized in his work, contrary to what might be expected. But grace must be received not only in the sacrament, it must be "acquired with much pain and labor"; it must be actualized, lived, and hence it must manifest itself and become perceptible in our spiritual life. "If the spring gushes up within us, the stream which proceeds from it must necessarily be visible to those who have eyes to see. But if all this takes

[16]*Sermon* 90. Ed. of Mount Athos (Russian), II, pp. 488-9.
[17]*Sermon* 45; ibid., I, pp. 414-16.

place within us without our having any experience or consciousness of it, it is certain that we shall then no longer feel the eternal life which is its result, that we shall not come to the light of the Holy Spirit, that we shall remain blind and insensible to eternal life, as well as being blind and insensible to our present life."[18] We cannot be truly Christians without having had the experience of light, a conscious communion with God. "We do not speak of things about which we are ignorant," says St. Simeon, "but we testify of that which is known to us. For the light already shines in darkness, in the night and in the day, in our hearts and in our minds. It illuminates us, this light that never sets, without change, unalterable, never eclipsed; it speaks, it acts, it lives and vivifies, it transforms into light those whom it illumines. God is light, and those whom he deems worthy of seeing him see him as light; those who have received him have received him as light. For the light of his glory precedes his face and it is impossible that he should appear otherwise than in light. Those who have not yet received it, who have not yet participated in the light, always find themselves still under the yoke of the law, in the region of shadows and images, they are still the children of the bond-woman. Kings or patriarchs, bishops or priests, princes or servants, people in the world or monks, they are all equally in darkness and walking in darkness if they are not willing to repent as they should. For repentance is the door which leads from the region of darkness into the region of light. Therefore those who are not yet in the light have not yet passed properly through the door of repentance (*Note:* the door of repentance takes the place of Origen's "door of gnosis").... The slaves of sin hate the light, fearing that it will expose their hidden works."[19]

In the light we know God, but we are also known and judged ourselves. For Evagrius the human spirit in self-

[18]*Sermon* 57, 4; ibid., II, p. 38.
[19]*Sermon* 79, 2; ibid., II, pp. 318-19.

contemplation appeared to itself as a god-like being; for Simeon it is our dissimilarity which is revealed above all in the divine light. "In the present life, when by repentance we enter freely and voluntarily into the divine light, we find ourselves accused and judged; however, by divine charity and mercy this accusation and judgment is made in secret, in the depth of our soul, for our purification and the pardon of our sins. It is only God and ourselves who see then the hidden depths of our souls. Those who undergo such a judgment in this life need no longer fear another trial. But for those who do not wish to enter into the light out of this world in order to be accused and judged, for those who hate the light, the second coming of Christ will reveal the light which has remained hidden up to then, and will make plain all that had been secret. Everything that we hide today, unwilling to disclose the depths of our hearts in repentance, will be exposed then in the light, before the face of God, before the entire universe, and what we are in reality will appear openly."[20]

The light is therefore a judgment, it is also the parousia already present for those who are living in communion with God, for the experience of uncreated light transcends the limits of created being; it is a departure out of time and space toward "the mystery of the eighth day." In this way mystical contemplation, in St. Simeon's doctrine, is connected with the eschatological vision.

In fact "for those who have become the children of light and sons of the day to come, for those who walk always in the light, the day of the Lord will never come, for they are already with God and in God. Therefore the day of the Lord will not appear to those who are already illumined by divine light, but will be revealed suddenly to those who live in the darkness of passions, to those who live after this world, attached to perishable goods. To such people this day will

[20]*Sermon* 57, 2; ibid., II, p. 37.

appear suddenly, unexpectedly, and it will be for them ter-
rible—like unbearable fire."[21]

In the deified state of the world to come the Holy Spirit
will appear in all things as light, but it is the person of
Christ which will be seen. "The grace of his Most Holy
Spirit," says Simeon, "will shine like a star upon the righteous
and in the midst of them thou wilt shine, thou, O Inaccessible
Sun! Then they will all be enlightened in the measure of
their faith and works, of their hope and charity, in the
measure of their purification and illumination by the Spirit,
O Only God of infinite forebearing."[22] "Christ will then be
seen by all and will himself behold the innumerable multitudes of saints, ceaselessly beholding each one in particular;
so that Christ will appear to each one as if he was looking
at him alone, directing his speech to him, welcoming him.
No one will be cast down, thinking that Christ has not known
him or that he has despised him. Always remaining un-
changed, Christ will show himself differently to each one.
He will enter into communion with each one, to the extent
that each is worthy of receiving him."[23]

We are tempted to say that this vision of God (which
is not a vision of the essence) has the character of an existential communion, if such a modern term can be applied to
the Byzantine spirituality of the eleventh century. Indeed
while it is a communion of created and uncreated natures
it is at the same time the glorious fulfilment [trans:
épanouissement] of each human person welcomed by God
as He addresses Himself to each one in particular. The words
of St. Paul: "I shall know him as I am known" acquire here
the meaning of a personal communion with a living God,
who is not only a universal nature but also the God of each.
It remains to be seen how this doctrine of the vision of God
found its dogmatic expression in the doctrinal conflict of
the fourteenth century.

[21]ibid.
[22]*Sermon* 27, trans. in *Vie Spirituelle* No. 27 (1931), p. 309.
[23]*Sermon* 52, 1. Ed. of Mount Athos (Russian), II, p. 479.

CHAPTER NINE

The Palamite Synthesis

The history of theological thought is composed of different periods or doctrinal cycles in which one aspect of the Christian tradition takes precedence over others, in which all doctrinal themes are treated to a certain extent as a function of the one question which has become central in the dogmatic consciousness. Not enough attention has been paid to the pneumatological coloring which Byzantine theology acquires more and more after the middle of the ninth century, after the final triumph over the iconoclasts, an epoch which marks the end of what may be called the Christological doctrinal cycle. Questions concerning the Holy Spirit and grace now form the nucleus around which theological thought will gravitate, a theology which is more than ever inseparable from spirituality. If in following Dionysius, St. Maximus and St. John Damascene developed a theology of deification inserted within the framework of a dynamic Christology, in the preceding chapter we have seen how this doctrine of deifying union was presented in a pneumatological aspect by St. Simeon the New Theologian. St. Simeon is indeed the "new theologian," for it is he who best expresses this pneumatological current in Byzantine thought, carried away by the mystery of the Holy Spirit dwelling in us, a thought which does not seek to be externalized, like Christological theology, but rather is wrapped in silence, in *hesychia*. A brutal intervention was necessary, a profanation of the mys-

tery of the hidden life of the contemplatives by certain representatives of a rationalistic theology, for this spirituality
of the cloisters and hermitages to come out of its isolation,
and, confronted by a doctrinal conflict, to attempt to express
itself dogmatically as a theology of mystical experience.

In 1339 the Calabrian monk Barlaam attacks the
Hesychasts of Mount Athos. He is not content to ridicule
their ascetical practices, but, basing his charge on the fact
that some of the Hesychastic monks were claiming to have
had the experience of uncreated light in which God reveals
Himself to contemplatives, a doctrine which we have seen
expressed by St. Simeon, Barlaam accuses them of Messalianism, of claiming a material vision of God. The debate
was centered on the nature of the light in which Christ
appeared to the apostles on Mount Tabor. Barlaam asserted
that this was a created phenomenon in the order of an at-
mospheric disturbance. A synod was assembled in Constantinople in 1431 where the question was stated on purely
dogmatic grounds. The question concerned the nature of
deifying grace. This involved all questions relative to the
possibility of really communing with God. The question
was that of our actual and not simply metaphorical deification, of the mode of our knowledge of God; it was the
question of the possibility of the mystical experience, the
question of the vision of God.

Several councils took place during the twenty years from
1340 to 1360, councils whose dogmatic importance and
teaching authority for the whole Orthodox Church in no way
yield to the authority and importance of the ecumenical
councils. St. Gregory Palamas was the spokesman of these
councils and the moving force in their dogmatic discussions.
He was born in 1296 and became a monk on Mount Athos
after a solid theological and philosophical education. Com-
pelled against his will to abandon the life of prayer in 1339
in order to take part in the dogmatic struggle, he became
Archbishop of Thessalonica in 1347, and died in 1359.

Canonized not long after his death, St. Gregory Palamas is given special veneration in the Orthodox Church: the second Sunday of Lent is consecrated to his memory.

Palamas' theological work has up to now not been properly appreciated in the West.[1] Those who have written about the doctrinal conflict of the fourteenth century, Fathers Jugie, Guichardan and Bois, have tended to regard "Palamism" (as they usually call it) as a dangerous heretical innovation, a break in the theological tradition of Byzantium. At the same time they have been forced to represent Palamas' adversaries as defenders of a tradition common to East and West. In reality, if we attempt to characterize the opponents of mystical theology in the light of the place they occupied in the social and cultural life of Byzantium, they appear to us to belong to a category of persons who cared very little about defending the Church's dogma. For the most part they were professors of rhetoric and humanists, who have never been lacking in Byzantium, men who were in love with the philosophy of antiquity, sometimes studying theological questions but more out of literary curiosity than out of concern for the truth. Already in the eleventh century the logician Michel Psellos had attempted to create a kind of scholasticism, but his disciple John Italos was condemned by the ecclesiastical authorities, and the rhetoricians will retreat to the study of philosophy and profane letters and will give up the attempt to encroach upon the realm of theology properly so called. With some reservations we can compare this intellectual world of Byzantium with that of the professors in the faculties of arts in the West, the world represented by such philosophers as Abelard, Siger of Brabant and William of Occam. But in

---

[1] The discovery and more fitting appreciation of St. Gregory Palamas by the West is now under way, thanks to the works of the Rev. Fr. John Meyendorff: *Introduction à l'étude de Gregoire Palamas*, Paris, 1959, Eng. trans. *A Study of Gregory Palamas*, London, 1964; and a critical edition of the *Défense des saints hésychastes* of St. Gregory Palamas, with introduction and notes, Louvain, 1959, 2 vols.

Byzantium, which knew no scholastic philosophy, the distance separating philosophers and theologians was greater. In the West St. Thomas Aquinas, for example, fought Averroism in the name of a Christian philosophy. In Byzantium in the fourteenth century philosophers who posed as theologians and attacked spirituality ran afoul of the dogmatic tradition. To regard the adversaries of St. Gregory Palamas simply as representatives of western thought, as "Byzantine Thomists," would be to distort many facts. There is here rather an encounter with Thomistic scholasticism on a somewhat intellectualistic level. But this intellectualism has eastern origins: overcome within theology, the old Hellenism reappears in the writings of the humanists who, formed by their studies of philosophy, wish to see the Cappadocians through the eyes of Plato, Dionysius through the eyes of Proclus, Maximus and John Damascene through the eyes of Aristotle. The question of the vision of God is posed on the intellectual level for the opponents of the Hesychasts—it is for them a gnosis, a knowledge; but for St. Gregory Palamas and the tradition of mystical theology which he represents it is inseparable from and constitutes one aspect of deification. The discussions center basically on the possibility of actual communion with God, i.e. on the nature of grace.

How can God's unknowable nature be reconciled with that which can be known in Him, His incommunicability with the possibility of actually communing with Him?

"The divine nature," says St. Gregory Palamas, "must be called at the same time incommunicable and, in a sense, communicable; we attain participation in the nature of God and yet he remains totally inaccessible. We must affirm both things at once and must preserve the antinomy as the criterion of piety."[2] St. Gregory Palamas resolves this antinomy, without suppressing it, by preserving the deep-rooted mystery which dwells intact within the ineffable distinction between the essence (οὐσία) and its natural energies.

[2]*Theophanes*. PG. 150, col. 932D.

"Illumination or divine and deifying grace," he writes, "is not the essence but the energy of God,"[3] "a power and universal operation of the Trinity."[4] Thus "while saying that the divine nature is communicable not in itself but in its energies, we remain within the limits of piety."[5] This distinction between essence and energies does not introduce any sort of division with the divine being. There would be a division if action was opposed to feeling, if energy presupposed a possibility (τὸ πάσχειν) in God; but God acts without suffering in relation to His action.[6] Essence and energies are not, for Palamas, two parts of God, as some modern critics still imagine, but two different modes of the existence of God, within His nature and outside His nature; the same God remains totally inaccessible in His essence—and communicates himself totally by grace. As with the dogma of Trinity, this dogma of divine energies in no way detracts from the simplicity of God, as long as simplicity does not become a philosophical notion which claims to determine the indeterminable. "It is right for all theology which wishes to respect piety to affirm sometimes one and sometimes the other, when both affirmations are true," says Palmas.[7] "Thus Sabellius, incapable of affirming that God is one and not one, because he saw only the unity of the substance, lost the notion of the Trinity of persons."[8] It is the same with the simplicity of God's nature and the distinction between οὐσία and energies. "God is not only in three hypostases, but he is also the All-powerful One—παντοδύναμος" (Council of 1351).

The distinction between οὐσία and energies or operations, as it is affirmed by the councils of the fourteenth cen-

---

[3]*Physical and Theological Chapters* 68-9; ibid., col. 1169.
[4]*Theophanes;* ibid., col. 941c.
[5]ibid., col. 937D.
[6]*Physical and Theological Chapters* 128 and 149; ibid., cols. 1212A and 1221C.
[7]ibid., 121, col. 1205.
[8]*Theophanes;* ibid., col. 917A.

tury, is the dogmatic expression of the tradition concerning the knowable attributes of God which we found among the Cappadocians, and later in the work of Dionysius in his doctrine of the divine unities and distinctions, of the powers (δυνάμεις) or the ray of divine darkness. This distinction gives rise to two theological paths with regard to the essence—affirmative and negative—the one revealing God, the other leading to union with God in ignorance. Finally, in the thought of St. Maximus and St. John Damascene, we have seen the same doctrine of energies applied to Christology and in particular to the communication of the divine glory to the human nature of Christ, in the hypostatic unity of the Incarnate Word. All these ideas of previous theology will serve, in the council of 1351, as the doctrinal basis for justifying the definition (in conformity with the tradition of the Fathers) which regards divine and uncreated grace as a distinct energy, and yet not separable from the one essence of the Trinity.

Palamas' opponents are defending a philosophical notion of the divine simplicity when they affirm the perfect identity of the essence and the energy of God. When they speak of operations and energies as distinct from the essence, they are thinking of created effects of the divine essence. Their notion of God—as simple essence—admits nothing but an essential existence for divinity. What is not the essence itself does not belong to the divine being, is not God. Therefore the energies must be either identified with the essence or separated from it completely as actions which are external to it, i.e. as created effects having the essence as their cause. A rationalistic doctrine of causality is introduced into the doctrine of grace. For the opponents of St. Gregory Palamas there was the divine essence, and its created effects, but there was no longer any room for divine operations or energies. Replying to his critics, St. Gregory Palamas confronted them with the following dilemma: either they must admit the distinction between essence and operation, but then their philosophical notion of simplicity would oblige them to reject the existence of the glory of God, grace and the light of the Transfiguration among creatures; or else they must categorically deny this distinction, which would oblige them to identify that which cannot be known with what can be known, the incommunicable with the communicable, essence and grace. In both cases the deification of created being and therefore also all actual communion with God would be impossible.[9]

This is what we find in the writing of one Nicephorus Gregoras, for example. For him the light of Mount Tabor was a form (μορφή), a figure (τύπος), a material symbol revealing the presence of the divinity, and nothing more.[10] The apostles on Mount Tabor beheld a reality belonging to the domain of beings (τίνα τῶν ὄντων), something knowable, therefore something created.[11] This assimilation of the knowable to the domain of being indicates in Gregoras a dependency on Dionysius, but on a Platonic Dionysius, seen through the eyes of Proclus and the neo-Platonic tradition, a Dionysius without the mainspring of his theological thought, that dynamic doctrine which would behold God revealing Himself ineffably in His δυνάμεις, communicating Himself and making Himself known. Not only men but angels too, according to Gregoras, can know God only by symbols and corporeal figures (διὰ συμβόλων καὶ τύπων σωματικῶν).[12] Here this philosopher, the adversary of Palamas, is strangely related to the Antiochene school, to John Chrysostom for example, for whom the angels know God before the Incarnation only in images and representations. But St. John Chrysostom admitted the vision of God in the person of the glorified Christ in the age to come, while for Gregoras the vision always remains within the category of a κατὰ διάνοιαν ὄψις—a vision within

[9]ibid., col. 929BC.
[10]PG. 149, col. 377.
[11]ibid., col. 384.
[12]ibid., col. 323.

thought. It is thought which in this world operates with symbolic representations, in order to extract concepts from them.[13] The immediate communion with God and all mystical experience remains impossible in this world and, in the age to come, it will be a purely intellectual knowledge, a beatitude of man's cognitive faculty. By way of philosophy Gregoras seems to have returned to the intellectualistic gnosis of Clement and Origen and to have impoverished it by depriving this intellectualism of its mystical character, by rationalizing it. Even when he turns to Dionysius he does so in order to prove, by playing on the term θεομίμησις, the imitation of God, the created character of deification, taken as a pious metaphor rather than an actual union of the created and uncreated.

Both parties hurl the accusation of Messalianism at each other. Palamas' opponents attempt to involve the vision of uncreated light in this accusation. The defenders of the divine energies treat as Messalianism the knowledge of the divine essence by the created intellect in the age to come; if no distinction is admitted between the essence and the revelatory energies, it is necessary to choose between intellectual Messalianism and the denial of all immediate communion with God.

What then is this uncreated light around which the theological debates of the fourteenth century revolve? It is the actual reality of the mystical experience about which St. Simeon the New Theologian had spoken with such insistence three centuries earlier: the perception of the grace in which God makes Himself known to those who enter into union with Him by transcending the limits of created being. In St. Gregory Palamas this mystical reality is rendered into the technical language of theology and inevitably undergoes in this process a certain doctrinal crystallization: "God is called light," he says, "not according to his essence,

[13]ibid., col. 393.

but according to his energy."[14] But if the energies can be called light, this is not just by analogy to material light (energy being propagated from a luminous source), but because they appear to contemplation as an ineffable reality for which the most suitable name is light. In so far as God manifests Himself and makes Himself known in His δυνά-μεις or energies, in His dynamic attributes, He is light. "The divine experience is given to each one according to the worthiness of those who experience it."[15] The perfect vision of divinity becoming perceptible as uncreated light, which *is* the divinity, is the "mystery of the eighth day," it pertains to the age to come, where we shall see God face to face. However, those who are worthy, those who are united with God, may come even in this life to a vision of "the Kingdom of God coming in power," as did the disciples on Mount Tabor.

The light which the apostles saw on Mount Tabor was not a created, meteorological phenomenon, as Barlaam said, a light inferior by nature to human thought. It was the light belonging by nature to God: eternal, infinite, uncircumscribed in time and space, existing outside created being. It appeared in the theophanies of the Old Testament as the glory of God, terrifying and unbearable for human creatures since before Christ it was external to men. This is why Paul, when he was still an outward man, alien to the faith in Christ, was blinded on the road to Damascus by the apparition of light. On the contrary Mary Magdalene was able to see the light of the Resurrection which filled the tomb and made everything in it visible, even though the "visible light" had not yet shone forth on the earth.[16] At the time of the Incarnation the divine light was as it were concentrated in the God-Man, in whom divinity dwelt bodily according to the word of St. Paul. It was this light of the

---

[14]*Against Akyndinos.* PG. 150, col. 823.
[15]*Hom.* 35. PG. 151, col. 448B.
[16]*Physical and Theological Chapters*, 67. PG. 150, col. 1169A.

divinity, the glory belonging to Christ by virtue of His divine nature, which the apostles were able to contemplate at the moment of the Transfiguration. The God-Man underwent no change whatsoever on Mount Tabor, but for the apostles this was a departure out of time and space, a glimpse of the eternal realities. "The light of the Transfiguration of the Lord," says St. Gregory Palamas, "has no beginning and no end; it remained uncircumscribed (in time and space) and imperceptible to the senses, although it was contemplated... but the disciples of the Lord passed here from the flesh into the spirit by a transmutation of their senses."[17]

Once again we find ourselves in a contradiction concerning the nature of this vision: on the one hand the divine light is imperceptible to the senses, on the other hand it is contemplated by the eyes of the body. St. Gregory Palamas indignantly rejects attempts to interpret his doctrine of vision in a material way: "The divine light is not material," he says, "there was nothing perceptible about the light which illuminated the apostles on Mount Tabor."[18] But on the other hand it would be absurd to assert that only intellectual gnosis merits the name of light, by way of metaphor.[19] This light is neither material nor spiritual, but divine, uncreated.

In the *Hagioritic Tome,* an apology for the Hesychasts written under the direction of St. Gregory Palamas, we find a very clear distinction between sensible light, intelligible light, and the divine light which surpasses the other two, both of which belong to the realm of created being. "The light of the intelligence," says the *Tomos,* "is different from that which is perceived by the senses. In fact perceptible light reveals to us objects which are subject to the senses, while intellectual light serves to manifest the truth that lies in thought. Therefore sight and intelligence do not perceive one and the same light, but it is fitting that each

[17]*Hom.* 35; op. cit., col. 433B.
[18]*Against Akyndinos.* PG. 150, col. 818.
[19]ibid., col. 826.

of the faculties should act according to its nature and within its limits. However, when those who are worthy receive grace and spiritual and supernatural power, they perceive by the senses as well as by the intellect that which is above all intellect ... how? That is known only by God and those who have had the experience of his grace."[20]

This shows us the true nature of Hesychastic contemplation, and also the place due to St. Gregory Palamas' theology, which crowns a long tradition of struggle to surpass the Platonic dualism of the perceptible and intelligible, sense and intellect, matter and spirit. Precisely because God transcends created being, because He is in essence absolutely inaccessible, because there is no co-naturality (συγγένεια) between the divine and the intelligible (made up of the angelic and human spirits), God makes Himself known to the whole man; were it not for this we could speak of a purely sensible or purely intellectual vision. Since the line of demarcation passes between the created and the uncreated and not between the perceptible world and the world of intellects conceived as related to the divine, the radical departure out of all created being is the only way—demonstrated by Dionysius—to attain the true knowledge of the living God. And this departure will no longer be a Platonic escape, a spiritualization of the human being as he is transformed into νοῦς, as with Origen and Evagrius. This will no longer be the "sense" mysticism of the Messalians. It will be neither the reduction of the sensible to the intelligible, nor the materialization of the spiritual, but a communion of the whole man with the uncreated One (we have already observed this in the doctrine of Dionysius and Maximus), a communion which implies a union of the whole human person with God "above all knowledge," "above the νοῦς," by surpassing the limitations of created nature. We are very far here from the Alexandrian spirituality, but are still very close to St. Irenaeus. The old anthropology gives

[20]PG. 150, col. 1233D.

way to a positive asceticism, not one of negating but of going beyond: "If the body must share with the soul the ineffable blessings of the age to come, it is certain that it must participate in them as far as possible from now on. . . . For the body itself also experiences divine things, when the passionate forces of the soul find themselves not put to death but transformed and sanctified."[21]

"He who participates in divine energy," Palamas again says, "becomes in some way light in himself; he is united to the light and with the light he beholds with all his faculties all that remains hidden to those who do not have this grace; thus he surpasses not only the corporeal senses but also all that can be known (by the intellect) . . . for the pure in heart see God . . . who as light dwells in them and reveals himself to those who love him, to his well-beloved."[22] This same uncreated light communicates itself therefore to the whole man, making him live in communion with the Holy Trinity. It is this communion with God, in which the righteous will be finally transfigured by light and will themselves become as resplendent as the sun, which constitutes the beatitude of the age to come—the deified state of creatures, where God will be all in all, not by His essence, but by His energy, i.e. by grace or uncreated light, "the ineffable splendor of the one nature in three hypostases."[23]

The *Hagioritic Tome* asserts that beside the dogmas of the Mosaic law the Old Testament contains prophetic previsions of the future dogmas of the age of the Gospel; these dogmas appeared to those who were faithful to the law before Christ as mysteries which could not be clearly expressed. In the same way for us, in the age of the Gospel in which we are now living, the realities of the age to come or the Kingdom of God are represented as mysteries. These

[21]*Hagioritic Tome.* PG. 150, col. 1233BD.
[22]*Hom. on the Presentation of the Virgin in the Temple.* Ed. Sophocles, pp. 176-7.
[23]*Hom.* 35. PG. 151, col. 448.

mysteries can be known or rather experienced in this world only by the saints, by those who, living in union with God, are transformed by grace and belong more to the age to come than to the life of this world.[24]

Thus under a new form we discover again the thought of St. Irenaeus, the progressive vision-revelation composed of three stages: before Christ, after the Incarnation, and after the Parousia. But the vision of the "paternal light" in this world was presented to St. Irenaeus in an eschatological perspective—the millenarian reign of the saints. This concept of an eschatological vision was replaced in the third century, as we have seen, by the Alexandrian ideal of the contemplative life which, in the doctrine of Clement and Origen, sometimes assumed the forms of a philosophical utopia, Clement's "gnostic man" and Origen's "spiritual man"—a spirituality of "escape" having origins alien to Christianity. This prompted certain modern critics (Nygren and, to some extent, Fr. Festugière) to assert that all mystical contemplation bears within itself the mark of a betrayal in relation to the only vision of God which conforms to the spirit of the Scriptures, the eschatological vision or Parousia. After centuries of struggle against intellectualistic mysticism we find in the writings of the Byzantine Hesychasts, in St. Simeon the New Theologian and in St. Gregory Palamas and his disciples, a vision-contemplation which is again connected with the eschatological vision: the departure out of history toward the eternal light of the "eighth day."

There is one further conclusion which we can draw. I have spoken of the violent criticism of the thought of St. Gregory Palamas in the work of Denis Petau. Leaving to one side the Greek Fathers of earlier epochs (accused also by Gabriel Vasquez for having denied the vision face to face since they did not profess the doctrine of the vision of the divine essence held by western scholasticism), Petau was especially infuriated by the Byzantine theology of the

[24]PG. 150, cols. 1225-7.

fourteenth century. According to him St. Gregory Palamas broke away from tradition by denying the immediate vision of God in order to replace it by the vision of something other than God—of a light separated from God, forming an uncreated world between the Trinity and uncreated beings. "An absurd doctrine," says Petau; but it ought to be clearly recognized that it is his own interpretation of Palamas' doctrine of energies which is absurd. He did not grasp the true meaning of this ineffable distinction which distinguishes another mode of the divine existence outside the essence of God, the mode of grace, in which God communicates Himself and manifests Himself. He did not see— and this is the great paradox—that all of Palamas' theological work constitutes a defence of the immediate vision of God, and that the distinction between essence and energy, far from being a separation or division of God into two parts, communicable and incommunicable, is an inevitable theological postulate if we wish to maintain the real and not just the metaphorical character of deification, without suppressing created being within the divine essence. Petau did not understand that this vision or knowledge of God face to face, in the light of His glory, was an uncreated vision and knowledge precisely because the distinction between essence and grace has its basis in God Himself; which eliminates the necessity of distinguishing between grace as the presence of God in us and grace as a created *habitus,* a distinction which can only be a separation. Petau and all the western critics who have followed him down to our own day—judging Byzantine theology from the standpoint of notions proper to Latin scholasticism—have been inclined to see a limitation, an impoverishment of the vision of God in the very place where on the contrary there was a Christian maximalism, one of the most daring affirmations of actual communion with God: the communion of the total man with God making Himself totally present. But this God is not an object of knowledge, He is not the God of the philosophers, but the

God who reveals Himself. If His essence, instead of manifesting itself in natural energies, were to become accessible and at a certain moment permit itself to be known in itself by the created intellect, this would not be, for St. Gregory Palamas and the tradition he represented, the knowledge to which mystical theology is aspiring, the vision which surpasses both intellect and senses, the vision which is a summons to the unceasing and infinite surpassing of created being.

Are we now in a position to reply to the questions raised by Gabriel Vasquez, who accused the majority of the Greek Fathers of having denied the vision of the divine essence? It is always difficult to prove the absence of a doctrine, especially when the doctrine is as subtle as this. The rapid survey which we have been able to make does not permit us to make a categorical reply which would relieve us of all further corrections and amendment.

However, we have been able to notice one fact: if there really is reference to a vision of God's essence in the writing of Clement of Alexandria and Origen, this doctrine (besides being poorly defined and poorly developed) is presented within the framework of an intellectualistic mysticism which opposes the sensible and intelligible and affirms the co-naturality of the intellect and the divine. The vision of the divine essence is then the crown of an intellectual gnosis.

On the level of spirituality we have found two opposing tendencies: on the one hand the Origenistic mysticism of Evagrius, where the intellect is by nature a receptacle of the essential light which perhaps (Evagrius does not say so explicitly) communicates to it a gnosis of the divine essence; on the other hand, the sensible participation in the essense of God of the Messalians. Orthodox spirituality is equally opposed both to intellectual gnosis and to the sensible perception of the divine nature, and seeking to surpass this dualism of the sensible and the intelligible within created being, it has tended toward a vision of God which draws the

whole man into the way of deification. This spirituality of
the surpassing of created being has gone hand in hand with
the categorical affirmation of the unknowable nature of the
essence of God: by Gregory of Nyssa, Dionysius, and
Maximus the Confessor. On the purely dogmatic level, the
reaction against the rationalism of Eunomius led to the
denial of the knowable nature of the divine essence by such
different theologians as the three Cappadocians, St. Ephraim
of Syria, St. Epiphanius and St. John Chrysostom. The doctrine of energies, first enunciated in the dispute with
Eunomius by St. Basil and St. Gregory of Nyssa, developed
by Dionysius as a dynamic notion of the divine attributes,
and reinforced by the Christological dynamism of Maximus
and John Damascene, served as the doctrinal basis for the
Byzantine theologians of the fourteenth century, who de-
fended the possibility of an immediate communion with God
while denying the gnosis of the divine essence. Another idea
is closely tied to the negation of the vision of the divine
essence in Byzantine theology: it is the distinction between
φύσις and πρόσωπον in the doctrine of St. Anastasius
the Sinaite, and the assertion that the face to face vision
is a vision of the person of the Incarnate Word. Against
the iconoclasts it was affirmed that it is not the divine or
human nature but the hypostasis of Christ which appears to
us in icons. The cult of icons will therefore be in a certain
sense the beginning of the vision of God. For St. Simeon the
New Theologian the face to face vision is a communion, a
kind of existential communion with Christ, where each person
in this communion finds his fulfilment, knowing God personally and being personally known and loved by God. This
vision of the luminous face of God turned toward each man,
the vision of Christ transfigured, is given its theological
structure in the doctrine of St. Gregory Palamas and in the
definitions of the nature of grace of the councils of the
fourteenth century.

   After several centuries we find ourselves confronted again

by the vision of Christ transfigured, through whom the Father communicates in the Holy Spirit the light of His inaccessible nature, a vision of God which we encountered at the outset of our study in the work of St. Irenaeus, father of the Christian tradition, disciple of St. Polycarp and also disciple of St. John, the one who said: "No one has ever seen God, the Son alone, who is in the bosom of the Father, has manifested him to us."

Index

Abelard, 15, 155
Abyss, 48, 50, 52, 54, 63, 73, 80
Action, 133, 143
Active life, 56, 107
Active way, 103
Adam, 69
Adoption, 29, 40, 70
Against Eunomius, 78
Against Heresies, False Gnosis Unmasked and Refuted, 36
Agape, 46, 88
Agnosticism, 20, 75
Albigensians, 15
Alexander of Alexandria, St., 73
Allegory, 45
Amalric of Bena, 15
Ambrose, St., 17
Ammonius Saccas, 67
Amphilochius, 78
Anastasius the Sinaite, St., 21, 137, 168
Annals of Love, 129, 132
Anomoeans, 18, 19, 75
Anthony, St., 103, 104
Aphraates, 91
Apophaticism, 48, 92, 129, 138
Archetype, the, 80-81
Arianism, 73, 75, 79
Aristotle, 156
Arius, 75
Armenians, doctrines of, 13, 15, 21, 22
Arnold of Brescia, 15
Ascension, 97
Asceticism, 66, 105, 106, 164
"Asceticism and Contemplation," 46
Ascetics, Christian, 89, 103
"Ascetikon," 112
Athanasius, St., 69-71, 98, 103
Athos, Mount, 154

Attributes, *see* Energies
Augustine, St., 32, 46
Autolycus, 33-35
Averroism, 156

Baptism, 34, 99, 112, 117, 148
Barlaam, Calabrian monk, 154, 161
Barsanuphius, St., 119
Basil, St., 17, 77-81, 83, 84, 94, 104, 105, 119, 122, 140, 168
Basil of Seleucia, 21
Beatitude, 11, 15, 23, 42, 43, 53, 82, 85, 88, 126, 160, 164
Benedict XII, pope, 12-13, 14, 21, 22
Benedictus Deus, 12-13
Bernard, St., 15
Bogomils, 111
Bois, Fr., 155
Boussuet, 30
Burning bush, 114

Cappadocian Fathers, 98, 131, 139, 156, 158, 168
Chiliastic doctrines, 45
Clement of Alexandria, 46, 47-55, 67, 68, 74, 80, 86, 89, 91, 97, 103, 122, 160, 165, 167
Cloud, 26
Commentaries and Discourses, 15
"Commentary on the Song of Songs," 87
Communication of idioms, 59
Communion, 69, 80, 135, 138, 140, 141, 151, 163; with God, 64, 71, 84, 88, 97, 109, 126, 131, 143, 147, 149, 150, 156, 159, 160, 166, 168; with the Holy Trinity, 100, 164
Comprehension, 19, 20

171